BEYOND BELIEF

Important Note

This book shares how the power of belief can change your life. To stay updated on new discoveries since publication and access practical tools to help you apply what you learn, I've prepared bonus companion resources for you.

Go to NirAndFar.com/belief-tools/
or scan the QR code below.

Also by Nir Eyal

Indistractable:
How to Control Your Attention and Choose Your Life

Hooked:
How to Build Habit-Forming Products

BEYOND BELIEF

The Science-Backed Way
to Stop Limiting Yourself and
Achieve Breakthrough Results

Nir Eyal

with Julie Li

PORTFOLIO · PENGUIN

Portfolio / Penguin
An imprint of Penguin Random House LLC
1745 Broadway, New York, NY 10019
penguinrandomhouse.com

Copyright © 2026 by Sunshine Development LLC
Penguin Random House values and supports copyright. Copyright fuels creativity, encourages diverse voices, promotes free speech, and creates a vibrant culture. Thank you for buying an authorized edition of this book and for complying with copyright laws by not reproducing, scanning, or distributing any part of it in any form without permission. You are supporting writers and allowing Penguin Random House to continue to publish books for every reader. Please note that no part of this book may be used or reproduced in any manner for the purpose of training artificial intelligence technologies or systems.

PORTFOLIO and PORTFOLIO with javelin thrower design are registered trademarks of Penguin Random House LLC.

Most Portfolio books are available at a discount when purchased in quantity for sales promotions or corporate use. Special editions, which include personalized covers, excerpts, and corporate imprints, can be created when purchased in large quantities. For more information, please call (212) 572-2232 or email specialmarkets@penguinrandomhouse.com. Your local bookstore can also assist with discounted bulk purchases using the Penguin Random House corporate Business-to-Business program. For assistance in locating a participating retailer, email B2B@penguinrandomhouse.com.

BOOK DESIGN BY TANYA MAIBORODA

LIBRARY OF CONGRESS CONTROL NUMBER: 2025043394

ISBN 9780593852033 (hardcover)
ISBN 9780593852040 (ebook)
ISBN 9798217185061 (international edition)

Printed in the United States of America
1st Printing

The authorized representative in the EU for product safety and compliance is Penguin Random House Ireland, Morrison Chambers, 32 Nassau Street, Dublin D02 YH68, Ireland, https://eu-contact.penguin.ie.

*For Ronit, Anne, Victor, and Paul—
who always believed.*

CONTENTS

1. **Beliefs Are Tools, Not Truths**
   How the beliefs you choose shape the life you live.   1

The First Power of Belief: Attention
The Power to SEE What You Believe

2. **Why Believing Is Seeing**
   Your brain isn't seeing reality—it's seeing your beliefs about reality.   17

3. **The Secret to Better Relationships**
   You don't have relationship problems. You have perception problems.   37

4. **How to See Opportunities Others Miss**
   Luck isn't chance.   59

The Second Power of Belief: Anticipation
The Power to FEEL What You Believe

5. **You Already Live in a Simulation**
   How to make the ordinary extraordinary (and make a fortune doing it).   79

6. **Sickness Is in the Body; Illness Is in the Mind**
   Not all pain is necessary.   99

7. **Living Longer, Stronger, and Smarter**
   Your beliefs can become your biology.   121

The Third Power of Belief: Agency
The Power to DO What You Believe

8. **How to Take Control of Your Life (Even When It's Impossible)**
   Believe you have control, even when you don't. — 143

9. **Prayer Works, With or Without Faith**
   Ritual is the bridge to your better self. — 161

10. **Your Labels Are Your Limits**
    Beware the beliefs that steal your power. — 187

Conclusion

11. **Good Beliefs, Bad Beliefs**
    Why your dreams might be sabotaging your goals— and what to do instead. — 207

Chapter Takeaways — 229

Acknowledgments — 255
Notes — 259

BEYOND BELIEF

CHAPTER 1

Beliefs Are Tools, Not Truths

How the beliefs you choose shape the life you live.

For much of my life, I was the kid who never took off his shirt at the community pool. While other teenagers splashed and played in the Central Florida summer heat, I'd sit on the edge, feet dangling in the water, wearing an oversized T-shirt to hide my belly rolls. On the rare occasions I mustered up the courage to get in, I still kept it on. Taking it off wasn't an option. Better to let the soaked garment cling to my boy breasts.

My friends wore jeans fresh from the mall, perfectly fitted and brand new but torn in all the right places. I wore hand-me-downs that needed to be shortened by half. I have painful memories of struggling into my overweight dad's old jeans, sucking in my gut until my ribs ached. No matter how I twisted or tugged, I couldn't hide the flesh spilling over the waistband.

Over the next thirty years, my bookshelf became a graveyard of diet books. In 1994, I meticulously logged fat grams in a worn spiral notebook, celebrating as the numbers on the scale dropped. Three years later, that notebook gathered dust while I filled my fridge with tofu and potatoes, convinced by passionate vegetarians that meat was the enemy. Then the pendulum swung. Foods I previously ate became contraband as I embraced low-carb, and then keto, preaching the gospel of metabolic flexibility. Eventually, I discovered intermittent fasting, which I believed was a new, higher state of being. Each new plan felt like the answer.

And in a way, each one was. I'd lose weight, feel better, and think I'd finally found the answer. I was the guy at parties who couldn't stop preaching about my latest diet revelation to anyone who would listen. Whether it was the evils of fat, the miracles of plant-based eating, or the magic of ketosis, I believed I'd found the "truth" of weight loss.

But every time, without fail, something awful would happen. I'd read an article or hear an expert explaining why my current diet was wrong. "Low-fat diets increase hunger." "Plant-based diets lack essential nutrients." "Ketosis damages your kidneys."

As my confidence faltered, so did my results. A new set of failure-justifying beliefs crept in along with the pounds. "It's hard for a bigger person to exercise," I'd tell friends. "The food-industrial complex is conspiring to keep us overweight. It doesn't matter what I eat." Without the guardrails of conviction, food choices became a free-for-all. I ate whatever I wanted, whenever I wanted. The pounds crept back on. Month after month, year after year, my weight graph traced the peaks and plunges of a roller coaster: rising, falling, and rising again.

Every diet worked... until it didn't. Every approach succeeded... until I abandoned it. There was a pattern here, something deeper than calories and carbs. Each success unraveled the same way, pointing to a cause I couldn't name. I kept looking in diet books for answers, unaware that the real explanation lay elsewhere entirely.

Hope Floats

In the 1950s, researcher Curt Richter conducted a groundbreaking, though ethically dubious, study.[1] Richter wanted to understand how stress affects survival, so he placed rats into tall glass cylinders filled with water and measured how long they could swim.

Richter tested both wild and domesticated rats. The wild ones were fierce, aggressive animals, recently trapped, constantly on the alert for any avenue of escape. They were stronger and, by nature, better swimmers. By any reasonable measure, they should have outlasted their tamer counterparts—but they didn't.

Every single one of the wild rats drowned within fifteen minutes. Some sank almost immediately. Richter found this baffling. These animals weren't physically incapable of swimming. Something else was happening.

When he tested domesticated rats, the results were dramatically different. The majority kept swimming for hours and hours, far outlasting the wild rats. This finding challenges our conventional wisdom about resilience. We often assume that "tougher" individuals, the ones with more strength or grit, naturally persist longer. Yet Richter's experiment suggested otherwise. The wild rats went under within minutes. The domesticated ones kept on fighting.

Although he could not know their thoughts, Richter suspected that the rats' survival depended, at least in part, on their mental state. In his notes, he offered an explanation. The wild rats, he wrote, "seem literally to 'give up.'" They displayed what Richter referred to as "hopelessness."

Having never been held or rescued, the wild rats interpreted their situation as inescapable. The domesticated rats, by contrast, having lived among humans throughout their lives, seemed to hold open the possibility that the situation might change. That slim difference in expectation, not any physical advantage, was what separated survival from surrender.

But Richter's study didn't stop there. He wanted to know: Could hopelessness be reversed?

Richter took a new group of wild rats, placed them in the water cylinder, and, just before they drowned, plunged his hand in and scooped them out. He held them briefly, allowing them to catch their breath as water dripped from their fur. After this momentary reprieve, back into the water they went. He repeated this process several times, teaching them that being placed in the water cylinder did not mean certain death.

Now, I'd like to ask you to guess how much longer these rats kept swimming.

I've often posed this question to audiences when discussing Richter's study. Remember, the first wild rats lasted only fifteen minutes. Most people expect the answer to be surprising. Many guess thirty minutes, perhaps even an hour. One hour? That's four times the original swim time and quite an ambitious guess!

Think of your own limits, the last time you pushed yourself to the edge. Maybe it was sprinting until your lungs gave out, focusing on a complex task until you were utterly spent, or tackling an overwhelming project. With that in mind, can you imagine anything that could make you go four times longer than your limit? Doubtful.

But here's the astonishing thing: The conditioned rats swam for sixty hours, some even longer. Not sixty *minutes*. Sixty *hours*. More than two and a half days of nonstop swimming. Richter found that wild rats, once conditioned, swam "just as long as domestic rats or longer."

"In this way," he wrote, "the rats quickly learn that the situation is not actually hopeless; thereafter, they again become aggressive, try to escape, and show no signs of giving up."

What changed? The rescued rats had learned a vital lesson: Persistence could lead to salvation. Escape was possible. That belief gave them a reason to keep swimming.

This profound difference wasn't physical. The rats' bodies hadn't changed. Something had shifted, as if a switch had been flipped from "why bother" to "keep going." Sixty hours of perseverance had been there all along. It just needed to be unlocked.

My Glass Walls

Richter's rats revealed something I'd been missing in my decades of dieting. It wasn't about finding the perfect plan. It was about belief.

When I truly believed in a diet—when I was convinced it would work—I followed through with near-religious devotion. Whether I was counting fat grams, carbs, or calories, it wasn't the diet rules that carried me forward, but my conviction that my effort mattered. But the moment doubt crept in, when I stopped believing, the commitment collapsed. Like Richter's rats, I let myself sink long before I reached my actual limits.

What I didn't see then was that a belief can be helpful without being universal or even strictly true. My all-or-nothing mindset, the idea that a diet was either entirely flawless or completely worthless, kept me stuck in a loop of rigid conviction and total abandonment. The real breakthrough came later, when I stopped chasing the "perfect" plan and started to believe that consistent daily choices over time mattered more than giant overhauls.

I stopped quitting and restarting. I experimented, adjusted, and continued to move forward. Instead of searching for the ideal answer, I began to notice which beliefs kept me going and which ones led me off track. Over time, those small, sustained changes added up to real, lasting results. True, I lost weight, built strength, and finally broke free from the endless cycle of yo-yo dieting. But the most important realization wasn't about food or fitness at all. It was that belief—not discipline or the particulars of the latest plan—is the real driver of sustained motivation.

Think of the last time you quit something that mattered to you. Maybe it was the book you started writing but never finished, the business idea you talked yourself out of, or the difficult conversation you've been avoiding for months. What story did you tell yourself in that moment of giving up?

"I'm not creative enough." "It's too late to start." "People like me don't succeed at this."

We repeat these phrases until they feel true. But they're not facts. What if these invisible barriers we've accepted are the very things keeping us from persevering longer than we ever thought possible?

The Missing Side of Motivation

Most people picture motivation as a straight line: If you want the benefit, you'll do the behavior. You do the work, you get the reward—simple cause and effect. But this model is incomplete.

Knowing what to do and why you should do it isn't enough. If it were, we'd all follow through on everything we know is good for us. You can have a perfect plan, backed by solid reasoning, but if you don't believe your effort will make a difference, you won't persist. And without that belief, even the best advice becomes wasted breath.

We are better off understanding motivation as a triangle. One side represents the actions you must take: your behavior. One side stands for the benefit: the outcomes you desire. And the bottom of the triangle, connecting the other two sides together, is your belief: your conviction that those actions will lead to the desired results.

THE MOTIVATION TRIANGLE

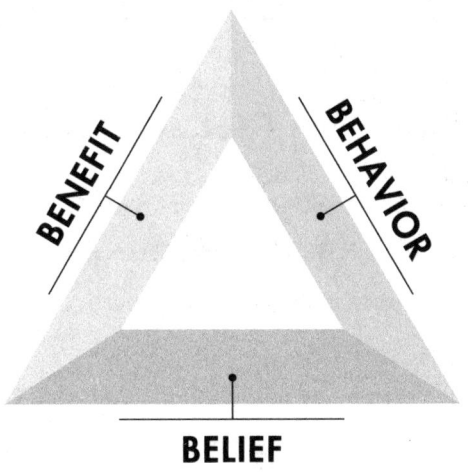

To sustain motivation, we must know what to do (behavior), know why we do it (benefit), and believe our actions will yield results (belief).

All three elements of the Motivation Triangle are essential, but belief is the foundation. Without belief, motivation collapses. Richter's rats revealed that beliefs matter. More importantly, his research showed that beliefs can be learned. That means that no matter how many times you've quit in the past, changes to your beliefs can make you stronger, more powerful, and more resilient than you ever imagined.

Why do people fail to accomplish their goals? There are countless answers to that question, but the one thing that assures failure is quitting. Of course, quitting isn't always wrong; I've quit many jobs, relationships, and projects. But success becomes impossible the moment you stop trying, the moment you give up like Richter's rats.

The most formidable obstacle to any meaningful change is rarely a lack of a good strategy or resources. We don't fail because we make mistakes; mistakes can be fixed. We fail because we quit, and we quit far more often, and far too soon, than is good for us.

What if we could change that?

Between Fact and Faith

Some things in life are certain. Water freezes at 0° Celsius. Light travels at approximately 300,000 kilometers per second. These are facts: measurable, verifiable, and true, whether one believes them or not.

At the other extreme is faith: a conviction that doesn't require evidence. Faith can be inspiring, but by definition, it doesn't ask for proof.

But most of life's essential questions happen in the vast, messy space between the two. Will this business succeed? Should I take this job? Is this the right person to marry? We can gather data, but we'll never have complete certainty. At one extreme, demanding absolute proof before acting risks analysis paralysis, and at the other, acting on pure faith and ignoring evidence risks getting blindsided. Our brains need shortcuts. We need working models of reality that help us make decisions without having perfect information. That's where belief lives: nestled between fact and faith.

Merriam-Webster defines a belief as "something that is accepted, considered to be true, or held as an opinion." Like any opinion, a belief can be informed by facts, but it doesn't require certainty. It's provisional—open to revision when new evidence arrives. And like any opinion, it is ultimately something we must individually choose to accept or reject.

Fact: An objective truth, verifiable through evidence.

Faith: A conviction without need for objective evidence.

Belief: A firmly held opinion, open to revision based on new evidence.

Think back to Richter's conditioned rats. Those that kept swimming had no assurance they'd be rescued again. What they had was a liberating belief: that their persistence might matter. And that belief, that firmly held opinion, powered their survival for days rather than minutes.

You've done the same. If you've ever pushed past a personal limit, whether it was running your first marathon, learning a new skill, or asking someone out without knowing they'd say yes, you acted without certainty of success. You moved forward because you believed your effort might make a difference.

In situations like these, it becomes especially clear that beliefs aren't simply thoughts or feelings. They're tools—working models we use to navigate reality when the truth isn't fully knowable. Like a carpenter choosing between a hammer and a saw, we can select beliefs based on how well they serve our goals. Similarly, we can choose beliefs based on their usefulness, rather than just their provability. "I can finish this marathon" may not be provably true, since plenty of people don't, but it's far more useful than believing "I can't."

Choosing a belief is a strategic decision, not self-deception. Scientists use simplified models to understand complex systems because they're useful for making predictions and guiding action. We can do the same with beliefs by adopting them to help navigate life's challenges while remaining open to new evidence. Beliefs are tools, not (necessarily) truths.

The real question isn't "Is this belief true?" but "Does this belief serve me?"

The best beliefs are both practical and adjustable. They offer just enough conviction to act, yet enough flexibility to adapt. They bridge the gap between paralyzed overthinking and blind faith.

This doesn't mean any belief is fair game. It's easy to slip from "choose the belief that serves you" into "believe whatever feels good," even if it contradicts evidence. Telling yourself, "I don't need to change; I can wish, manifest, or wait for things to fix themselves," might feel comforting, but it's often an excuse for inaction. A truly useful belief helps you grow and meet reality with more skill and resilience, rather than wishing it away.

This book is a staunch rejection of magical thinking and blinding denial. A belief is only a good tool if it

- holds up to real-world feedback,
- remains open to revision, and
- doesn't require ignoring evidence to sustain it.

If a belief makes you temporarily happier but leads you away from truth, healthy action, or growth, it's not helping you—it's harming you. Beliefs worth keeping must be both valuable and reality-tested, not just comforting.

The Shortcomings of "Just Believe"

When I finally lost the weight and kept it off, it wasn't because I'd found the perfect diet. It was because I'd found the right liberating beliefs: not just about food or exercise but about myself and what was possible. The specific eating plan mattered less than my deep conviction that I could change and that my actions would eventually yield results.

This principle applies far beyond weight loss. The writer who finishes their first novel, the musician who finally performs on stage, and the executive who successfully leads a team through a crisis all succeed not because they discovered secret techniques, but because they developed beliefs that sustained their efforts through inevitable setbacks. Whether you're trying to advance your career, build meaningful relationships, or master a craft, the right beliefs provide the foundation that makes persistent action possible.

So, is the answer simply to "just believe"? Absolutely not.

The "think positive" and "just believe" mantras we've all heard are not exactly wrong, just incomplete. They acknowledge that beliefs matter but offer no practical way to build them. They treat beliefs as something you either have or don't, like a mysterious quality you can turn on or off at will.

The truth about belief is both more practical and more powerful. Beliefs aren't wishes or manifestations; they are mental models built through experience, evidence, and deliberate construction. Just as you wouldn't expect to develop physical strength without training, you can't develop powerful beliefs without strategic and consistent effort.

If belief is the foundation of motivation, how do you strengthen it?

The Three Powers of Belief

In the chapters ahead, you'll see how this works in real life: how people in wildly different situations have used belief to transform what seemed impossible into reality. You'll meet a man who undergoes orthopedic surgery without anesthesia by shifting his beliefs. You'll see how an entrepreneur built a $100 million business and helped thousands of unhoused individuals get back on their feet. You'll discover why placebos work even when we know they're fake and how beliefs about aging can predict longevity better than traditional health markers.

Each story illustrates one of the Three Powers of Belief: attention, anticipation, and agency.

1. **Attention: The Power to SEE What You Believe**
   We've been told that "seeing is believing," but studies show the opposite is just as true: Believing is seeing. You'll learn how beliefs shape perception, why attention is the gateway to possibility, and how to train your mind to notice opportunities others miss.

2. **Anticipation: The Power to FEEL What You Believe**
   Beliefs act as emotional forecasts, shaping your energy, mood, and performance. You'll explore the science of placebos, the psychology of expectation, and how to design beliefs that pull you forward instead of holding you back.

3. **Agency: The Power to DO What You Believe**

    This is the power that turns belief into sustained action, even in the face of uncertainty. You'll see how ancient rituals, modern neuroscience, and mental training can help you stay motivated when most people give up.

Together, these three powers—attention, anticipation, and agency—create a robust framework for lasting change. They offer a new way to respond when things get hard, when progress stalls, or when doubt creeps in. Most importantly, they'll show you how to turn belief into your most reliable tool for a happier, healthier, and more prosperous life.

Of course, not all beliefs are created equal. Every day, millions of people fight invisible battles with their own beliefs. They want to improve their health, relationships, and careers, but feel stuck—not because they lack effort, but because they've internalized limits that don't actually exist.

These limiting beliefs subtly hinder our capabilities, whispering, "This won't work." "I'm not cut out for this." "I'll fail again." If we leave those harmful notions unexamined, we start to think they're true and allow them to restrict what we think is possible.

Fortunately, beliefs can change. And once you know how to replace a limiting belief with a liberating one, you can transform not just how you think but what you see, how you feel, what you do, and ultimately who you are.

FROM LIMITING BELIEFS...	TO LIBERATING BELIEFS...
Incentives (like rewards and punishment) are enough to motivate people.	Motivation requires knowing what to do (behavior), the desired outcome (benefit), and the conviction that actions will lead to results (belief).
I need to be certain of my beliefs.	I can choose beliefs based on usefulness, not certainty.
I should firmly defend my beliefs and never give them up.	Beliefs are not facts or faith. They are firmly held opinions, open to revision based on new evidence.
I should wait until I have as much information as possible before acting.	I can act with imperfect information and learn as I go.
When something is difficult, it means I'm not cut out for it.	Difficulty is evidence of growth. Struggle means I'm getting better.
If I've failed before, it's because I'm naturally bad at it and will likely fail again.	Each attempt teaches me something that increases my chances of future success.
I need to find the right approach before I begin. It's not worth continuing if I'm doing it wrong.	Progress comes from consistent action, not perfect plans.

THE FIRST POWER OF BELIEF

ATTENTION

> The
> Power to
> **SEE**
> What You
> Believe

We do not see things as they are, we see them as we are.
—FREQUENTLY ATTRIBUTED TO ANAÏS NIN

CHAPTER 2

Why Believing Is Seeing

Your brain isn't seeing reality—it's seeing your beliefs about reality.

T HE SURGEON'S SCALPEL sliced through the skin of Daniel Gisler's ankle as he lay fully conscious on the operating table. No anesthesia. No painkillers.

Most people would have been overwhelmed with agony as the surgical team wrenched metal screws from bone. Gisler, remarkably, felt almost nothing. Just three hours earlier, the fifty-six-year-old former derivatives executive had arrived at a Swiss hospital for a procedure that typically demands full sedation. Gisler refused it. His only shield against pain was the guidance of a fellow hypnosis student, someone he'd met just months before, and his conviction that his mind and beliefs could control what he felt.

The surgeon watched in disbelief as Gisler, fully awake and unmedicated, drifted somewhere beyond the boundaries of pain. He was aware of the pressure, the tugging, even the scraping of metal inside his body. But in his mind, he was somewhere else entirely.

The remarkable thing about Gisler's case is how *unremarkable* it actually is. Gisler's surgery is among the thousands of similar procedures performed in European hospitals, particularly in Belgium and France, where the medical community increasingly accepts this approach. Gisler's experience is just one data point in a growing body of evidence supporting the effectiveness of *hypnosedation*.

Brain imaging studies show that hypnosedation is not mere relaxation and has little to do with the stage-show version of hypnosis most of us imagine. The technique fundamentally alters the way the brain processes sensory information. Scientists studying patients under hypnosedation have observed measurable changes in brain activity, particularly in the regions responsible for pain perception and executive control.[1]

As the surgeon continued with the operation, Gisler's vital signs remained surprisingly stable. No spike in heart rate, no sudden increase in blood pressure. These physiological measures would typically surge in response to intense pain. Yet patients undergoing surgery with hypnosis show significantly more stable vital signs throughout their procedures. Similarly, their muscles remain more relaxed, making the surgeon's job easier, and they experience substantially less postoperative inflammation.[2] In a study comparing thyroid surgery patients, those who used hypnosedation returned to work after an average of just ten days, compared to thirty-six days for those who had received general anesthesia.

During the nearly hour-long procedure, Gisler's hypnosis training partner guided him deeper into his trance. Gisler recalled, "She'd say, 'go deeper, go deeper.' And so I opened a wormhole, which I remembered from a movie with Jodie Foster, *Contact* . . . where she's going through that wormhole to different places. So I did that and landed on this white beach with the deep blue sea."[3]

What allowed Gisler to transport his mind and tune out unbearable pain? And what does hypnosedation reveal about the extraordinary power of belief to shape our perception?

Consider your troubles for a moment. What ails you—physically, emotionally, financially? What challenge in your life could possibly compare to having metal screws extracted from your leg, fully awake, without anesthesia?

If beliefs can nearly erase real, physical suffering, what other boundaries might they help you cross? How much of your pain, whatever its source, is truly unavoidable, and how much is a matter of where you focus your mind?

Surgery without anesthesia isn't something most of us would consider, and that's not what this chapter is asking of you. However, the fact that thousands of ordinary people, like Daniel Gisler, have successfully undergone major procedures this way reveals something profound about human potential: We can reshape our perception of reality by directing our attention through the power of belief. While hypnosedation requires special training, the core principle that changed Gisler's experience is universal. What follows is your practical guide to developing this remarkable ability—one that will help you push through discomfort, sustain motivation, and transform your life.

Life Through a Keyhole

Your conscious mind can handle around fifty bits of data every second.[4] This is roughly equivalent to reading one short sentence per second, or just enough information to process a simple thought or instruction.

It seems like a reasonable amount of information to hold in your head at any moment. But compare that to the eleven million bits of total raw data collected by your senses in the same amount of time. That's the equivalent of seeing every word of *War and Peace* flash before your eyes twice per second.

Consider those two numbers: fifty bits versus eleven million bits. The gap between those two numbers is why we're aware of only a tiny fraction of what our brains can actually perceive. In short, we live life through a keyhole. This extreme filtering is why two people can witness the exact same event and walk away with entirely different experiences. Your conscious mind isn't receiving an objective recording of reality—it's getting an extraordinarily condensed highlight reel, curated by your nonconscious, based on what your beliefs flag as important.[5]

Take a moment and look around. Notice how your attention jumps from object to object? See if you can simultaneously focus on the sensation of your breath, the ambient sounds in your environment, and the words on this page. You'll quickly discover it's impossible. Don't feel bad. Your brain creates a convincing illusion that you're fully aware of everything happening around you. It feels like you're "taking it all in"—experiencing all eleven million bits of incoming data flowing in every second. But you're not.

Your attention constantly shifts among different inputs—touch, smell, taste, sight, and sound—like a surveillance system cycling between security cameras. You don't notice the switching because it happens so seamlessly.

Sometimes this narrowing goes even further. You can become so absorbed in one thing that everything else disappears entirely. Have you ever driven while listening to an audiobook, only to realize you don't remember the last few miles? Or gotten so captivated by a video on your phone that you completely lost awareness of your body until your arm went numb?

I've experienced this phenomenon countless times. When writing this book, I would sometimes become so engrossed that I'd suddenly realize hours had passed without any awareness of hunger, even though I'd worked straight through meals. My work made it through the keyhole; hunger signals did not. To be clear, the hunger was there. I just didn't experience it.

This clever, constant, and essential filtering process gives rise to your faculty of attention. It's the spotlight your nonconscious brain uses to illuminate a narrow slice of input, just enough for your conscious mind to feel like it's seeing the whole picture.

But how does the nonconscious decide what to reveal? It filters based on what matters.

And how does the brain know what matters? That's where things get *really* interesting.

Redirecting Attention

"If somebody had told me maybe even five years ago about hypnosis, I would have said that's crazy stuff," Gisler told me. Like most, he'd believed that pain was unavoidable. This wasn't just an opinion; it was a fundamental assumption about reality itself, one that shaped what he perceived as possible. But after hearing a friend rave about a hypnosis course he'd taken, curiosity led Gisler to challenge his mental models. He found some instructional videos on YouTube and began experimenting with light hypnotic states himself.

These early experiences created small but significant moments of surprise for his brain: The impossible was now happening. His mind was forced to confront the contradiction between "hypnosis can't work" and "I just experienced something unusual while watching these videos." He began to update his beliefs.

Intrigued, Gisler began training with a reputable local hypnosis instructor. During training sessions, Gisler and his classmates took turns experimenting with their tolerance for minor pain. He would grip a surgical artery clamp (a stainless steel instrument that looks like scissors but with blunt, ridged jaws instead of blades) and deliberately pinch folds of his skin. Without hypnosis, the pain would trigger an instinctive flinch. In his altered state, however, Gisler observed the metal teeth pressing into his flesh with detached curiosity. If he closed his eyes, he'd have to open them just to verify the clamp was indeed biting into his skin.

Each successful test of hypnosedation strengthened new neural pathways, rewriting his beliefs about pain. After only weeks of preparation, he felt ready for his anesthesia-free ankle surgery.

In the popular misconception, hypnosis looks like a zombie-like trance of extreme suggestibility, complete with swirly pinwheel eyes. In reality, the practice does not involve surrendering control over one's attention but rather achieving *heightened* control over it. Hypnosis empowers the mind to direct attention with extraordinary precision, spotlighting specific bits of information while allowing others, such as pain, to fade into the periphery.

For Gisler, the technique worked remarkably well—until the final moments. Near the end of the procedure, he heard the surgeon say, "Just ten minutes remaining." It was a routine comment for a surgeon to make, but it was this surgeon's first time operating on a patient under hypnosedation. By indicating the procedure was nearly over, he had unknowingly cued Gisler to ease up from his state of intense focus. "That was my biggest mistake," Gisler told me.

When Gisler opened his attentional aperture, he began to notice sensations he had been previously unaware of. He'd felt no pain when the surgeon carved through tissue and pried metal from living bone, but now he noticed something surprising. "Those final tiny stitches actually hurt the most." Those were ten difficult minutes. "The biggest lesson learned," Gisler said, "was only come out of hypnosis when it's really, really, *really* finished."

Gisler's remarkable experiences demonstrate how redirecting attention away from pain can alter our perception of it. But when Gisler broadened his keyhole of attention, the pain flooded back. The shift wasn't physical. It was perceptual.

A new belief had taken root, giving Gisler seemingly superhuman abilities. Attention doesn't just observe reality—it shapes it. It amplifies what we focus on while diminishing what we ignore. Pain is not objective. This doesn't mean pain is imaginary, however. Instead, Gisler's experience demonstrates how the power of attention, shaped by belief, can influence the intensity of our pain. The tens of thousands of patients who have successfully used hypnosedation show us that suffering is not inevitable.

You Can't See the Truth

Unfortunately, not all beliefs can be changed in the same way Gisler was able to rewire the relationship between attention and pain. Some beliefs are so deeply ingrained that they become impossible to change. Consider your lying eyes, for instance.

Look at the chessboard and cylinder below.[6] At first glance, the squares labeled A and B appear to be different colors. But they're not. If we isolate the precise color of each, we see that they're the exact same shade.

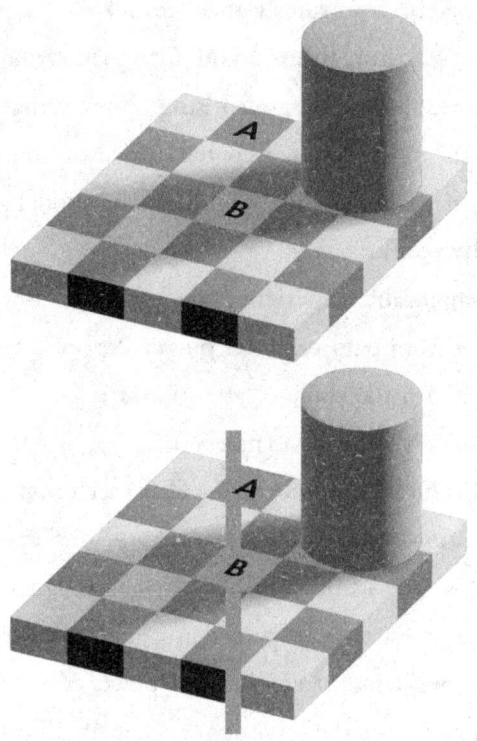

In the top image, square A is darker than square B, right? Squares A and B are the same color, but your brain won't let you see it any other way in the top image, even when you know the truth.

You'd expect an illusion or two in a pop-psychology book, but the interesting part is what comes next. Even though you now know that squares A and B are the same shade, square A still looks darker than B. No matter how many times you compare the two squares, you cannot force your mind to see the truth. Your brain simply won't let you. But why?

Your brain doesn't passively record reality like a camera. It actively constructs a version of reality for you. To do so, it relies heavily on your prior beliefs.

In the case of the illusion above, your brain "knows" that checkerboards alternate between light and dark squares, and it "knows" that shadows make things appear darker than they really are. Armed with these scripts, your visual system automatically adjusts what you perceive, making it impossible to see the identical shades as the same.

Think about the last time you had a heated argument with your partner, perhaps over something as mundane as household chores. You go to get a glass of water and your spouse says, "All the glasses are in the sink." You perceive their tone as accusatory and their timing as deliberately inconsiderate after your exhausting day. Within minutes, unkind words are returned, and you're in a full-blown argument. Meanwhile, your partner is genuinely confused by your defensive reaction, believing they simply made a neutral statement of fact.

Despite experiencing the same thirty-second interaction—the same words, the same environment—you each walk away with an entirely different perception of what happened. You're sure they were attacking your character; they're equally sure they were saving you from a waste of time. Neither of you is lying or deliberately misremembering; your different beliefs about each other's intentions created two different versions of an identical conversation.

There's a reason why these kinds of arguments are so difficult to resolve (and why marriage counselors stay in business). Even when you want to see things from the other person's perspective—even when you admit they have a point—it's not that easy. As with the checkerboard illustration we just saw, an illusion can still keep its hold on you *even when you know it's an illusion.*

This isn't a flaw of perception; it's how perception fundamentally works. Because conscious attention has limited bandwidth, your brain must rely on beliefs to fill in gaps, make predictions, and construct a usable model of reality.

The checkerboard illusion reveals we don't see reality as it is; we see reality as our beliefs tell us it *should* be. So perhaps the saying "I'll believe it when I see it" would be more accurately stated as "I'll see it when I believe it."

Seeing Problems That Don't Exist

Our perceptual mechanism works in both directions. Just as our beliefs can help us selectively ignore sensations that would normally overwhelm us (like pain in surgery without anesthesia), they can also prompt us to see things that aren't actually there and create problems where none exist.

In a series of revealing experiments, Harvard psychologist David Levari showed how our definitions and standards can shift without us realizing it. In one study, participants were shown eight hundred faces with expressions ranging from very angry to completely neutral. Their task was to identify the "threatening" ones. Initially, the mix included many threatening expressions, making the task straightforward. After the first two hundred images, however, Levari reduced the number of threatening faces.

Rather than correctly noticing there were fewer angry expressions, participants began categorizing neutral expressions as threatening. In other words, their judgment adjusted to find more of what they'd been led to expect, even when it wasn't there. They believed that threatening faces were all around, and they unconsciously modified their definition of "threatening" to adhere to that belief. Levari's research subjects had been trained to see threats where none existed.

In another experiment, participants were shown dots ranging from very purple to very blue; their task was to identify only the blue ones. As researchers gradually reduced the number of completely blue dots, participants began categorizing dots with more and more red in them as "blue," even though they were purple.

The same pattern was observed when participants were asked to evaluate research proposals for ethical concerns. As the frequency of genuinely unethical proposals declined, participants started flagging acceptable ones as problematic.

Each time, the participants might have updated their beliefs when presented with new evidence. *The faces are getting less threatening. The dots are getting less blue. The proposals are getting more ethical.* But they didn't. Instead, they intuitively adjusted their definitions of "threatening," "blue," and "ethical" to align with their expectations.[7]

The same phenomenon explains why, even when conditions in society improve, we can fail to recognize that progress. Take the hot-button topic of crime. From 1993 to 2019, violent crime in the United States decreased by 49 percent. Property crime decreased even more sharply. However, in nearly every survey of Americans conducted over the same period, large majorities reported that crime was increasing year after year.[8] As violent crimes decrease, we expand our definition of what constitutes a violent crime. As one study explained, "When problems become rare, we count more things as problems."[9]

The implications for everyday life are profound. If you've come to expect people to be cruel rather than kind, you'll notice more cruelty. If the news you consume is filled with stories of violence and hate, you're likely to perceive threats in neutral situations. The dissatisfaction we all periodically feel isn't necessarily a reflection of reality. More often, it's our brains creating problems *because* none exist.

Since perception follows beliefs, we perceive the problems we look to find, and if we can't find them, our brain skews the data to fit the brief. If you believe your partner is constantly criticizing you, innocent comments transform into attacks. If you believe your boss doesn't value you, any feedback becomes proof of your perceived inadequacy. This cycle becomes especially dangerous when it reinforces our negative beliefs, locking us into a belief-driven feedback loop that distorts reality and quietly builds a prison of our own making.

Rumination Magnifies Problems

Maria is a talented software engineer I met while researching this book. After a critical comment from her manager about a presentation she'd made, Maria found herself trapped in what psychologists call *rumination*: the tendency to repeatedly focus attention on negative thoughts, feelings, or experiences.

"For weeks after that feedback, I couldn't think of anything else," Maria told me. "I'd walk out of meetings where I'd contributed valuable ideas, but all I could remember were the moments I stumbled over words. I'd receive emails praising aspects of my work, but my mind would immediately jump to that one critical comment and what it might mean about my competence." Maria's belief that she was "bad at presenting" created a perceptual filter that transformed what she could see and remember. Reality offered her plenty of evidence to challenge that belief, but she wasn't seeing it. Her brain was filtering it out.

The stakes were higher than Maria initially realized. As her belief solidified, she began declining opportunities to present her work, even when senior leadership specifically requested her insights. "I turned down a chance to demo our team's work to the CEO," she admitted. "My manager was shocked—it was a career-making opportunity. But all I could think about was how I'd embarrass myself."

Her avoidance strategy backfired spectacularly. By refusing to present, Maria inadvertently reinforced her manager's concerns about her communication skills. During her performance review, she was passed over for a promotion she'd worked toward for two years. The feedback? "Technical skills are exceptional, but this employee needs to develop executive presence and communication abilities."

"The irony," Maria said, "was that I'd actually given dozens of successful presentations before that one critical comment. But once I believed I was bad at it, I created a reality where it became true."

The effects of rumination are evident in physical changes on brain scans. Test subjects in one study who were asked to ruminate on negative thoughts showed increased activity in the *default mode network*, the areas of the brain involved when the mind wanders or focuses inward.[10] In people prone to depression, this network connects strongly to the subgenual prefrontal cortex, a region linked to negative emotions and depressive thoughts. In other words, habitual rumination strengthens brain patterns that keep you stuck and unhappy.[11] Over time, those negative habits of mind can turn into an increased risk of clinical depression.[12]

When you ruminate, you selectively direct your attention toward evidence that confirms your negative beliefs while filtering out contradictory information. If you believe "I'm unlikable," your attention automatically spotlights each awkward social interaction, while positive encounters get filtered out. As you attend more closely to the evidence supporting your negative belief, the belief only becomes stronger—a vicious cycle.

What makes rumination particularly insidious is that it feels "productive," as though you're figuring out something important. In reality, you're not solving much. Instead, you're strengthening the neural pathways that amplify problems, or even create them from thin air.

"I thought I was being analytical and thorough by reviewing what went wrong," Maria told me. "But I was actually training my brain to only see evidence that confirmed my worst fears."

Rewriting Rumination

Now, you might be thinking: "So you're telling me that I should simply stop thinking about my problems, and they'll just magically go away?" Not exactly.

Maria's struggles were real—she lost out on a promotion and damaged her career trajectory. But here's what matters: While she couldn't change what happened in that presentation, she could change how her brain interpreted it going forward.

Think back to the checkerboard illusion. Your eyes insist squares A and B are different colors, even when you *know* they're identical. You're holding two truths at once—*what you see* and *what you know*. This is exactly how belief change works.

Maria's gut screamed, "I'm terrible at presenting!" just as convincingly as your eyes see those different shades on the board. Her racing heart and sweaty palms felt like proof. But feelings aren't facts, just like your visual perception of the checkerboard isn't accurate.

Unlike the visual illusion that stays locked in place, you can update your beliefs about yourself. Maria could acknowledge "I had one rough presentation" without accepting "I'm a bad presenter" as her identity. One is a reflection on a single event; the other is a limiting belief about her fundamental abilities.

The question isn't whether Maria's presentation went poorly. Maybe it did. The question is: Which belief serves her better moving forward?

Beliefs are tools, not truths. Holding on to "I'm terrible at presenting" guarantees Maria will see only evidence supporting that view, subsequently creating the exact reality she feared.

Instead, Maria made a choice. She decided to act on evidence rather than anxiety, just as you can choose to trust the illustration showing that the checkerboard squares are identical, rather than your lying eyes.

But beliefs don't change by themselves. They require intentional strategies to pull your attention away from old narratives and redirect it toward something more useful. Here are techniques shown to help:

- **Prove yourself wrong.** Beliefs are opinions that are open to revision in the face of new evidence. One tactic is to deliberately seek evidence that weakens your limiting beliefs, challenging your negative narratives by looking for contradictory evidence.
    - Maria decided to create what she called a "reality log." For two weeks, she documented every interaction related to her communication skills—not just the stumbles but also the successes. "I was shocked," she told me. "In just two weeks, I had logged seventeen positive interactions about my work explanations, three neutral ones, and only two that were genuinely negative." The evidence had always been there, but her belief had filtered it out. By forcing herself to track both types of feedback objectively, she gradually retrained her attention to see a more complete picture. "It was like switching from a

funhouse mirror to a regular one," Maria said. "The distortion disappeared once I started looking for the full truth, not just the parts that confirmed my fears."

- **Create distance.** Psychologists recommend a technique known as *illeism*: talking about yourself in the third person. When Maria found herself spiraling after a team meeting, she tried this approach. Instead of thinking, "I just made a fool of myself when I couldn't answer that question," she reframed it as, "Maria got caught off guard by an unexpected question. It happens to everyone." She even started journaling this way: "Maria had a challenging day. She presented the quarterly road map, and while most of it went smoothly, she's fixating on the thirty seconds where she lost her train of thought."

    It sounds ridiculous, but research shows that self-distancing works. This linguistic shift creates cognitive distance, enabling us to view our situations with the same wisdom we'd offer a friend.[13] When people refer to themselves in the third person during emotionally challenging situations, it helps them stay calmer.[14] Brain scans show that this trick quiets down the parts of the brain that make us act impulsively, without requiring extra mental effort.[15] "The third-person thing felt silly at first," Maria admitted, "but it immediately made my problems feel more manageable—like I was advising a friend instead of drowning in my own anxiety."

- **Question your motives.** Each time Maria caught herself replaying that original critical feedback, she'd pause and ask, "Is thinking about this for the fifteenth time today helping me improve, or just making me feel worse?" This metacognitive (thinking about thinking) approach helped her recognize when rumination was masquerading as problem-solving.

- "I realized I'd spend hours analyzing a two-minute interaction," she said, "convincing myself I was 'learning from it' when really I was just deepening the groove of self-criticism." She started setting a five-minute timer when she caught herself ruminating. "I'd give myself exactly five minutes to extract any useful lessons, write them down, then deliberately shift my attention to something else. After a few weeks, I noticed I needed the timer less and less—my brain was learning that endless analysis wasn't actually productive." When you find yourself stuck in a negative loop, step outside the internal debate for a moment to question the usefulness, not just the truth, of what you're ruminating about.

Unlike positive thinking or simple denial, practices like these work by helping you recognize and replace the beliefs filtering your attention. By changing how you talk to yourself about challenges, you change what your brain prioritizes as important information.

Your attention is a spotlight illuminating a tiny fraction of all the available information. If that spotlight is guided by the belief that "I must analyze why I keep failing," you get more evidence confirming exactly why you're inadequate. If you adopt the belief that "gaining perspective helps solve problems," you redirect that spotlight toward a more balanced and constructive reality, where you can see both challenges and potential solutions more clearly.

Seeing Beyond Limits

Belief defines what we think is possible. Before his hypnosedation training, Gisler would have considered surgery without anesthesia impossible. Yet there he was, redirecting his attention away from the operating table and toward his beach scene, accomplishing what he once thought couldn't be done. He had learned to control his attention so precisely that it changed what his mind experienced.

While his story is extreme, the principle applies far beyond surgery. We all do the same thing every day. Sometimes we redirect our attention away from discomfort. Other times, we fixate on what we fear and unconsciously create the very outcomes we want to avoid. That's what Maria learned and what the studies of perceptual illusions and societal misconceptions discussed above make clear: We don't passively see reality—we assemble it. And what we assemble depends on what we believe.

This is the First Power of Belief in action. Once you understand attention, you can use it to reshape how you experience challenges, handle relationships, and see yourself.

The following chapters will show you how to put your beliefs to work. First, we'll examine the beliefs we bring into our interactions with others. You'll learn how I transformed a strained relationship with my mother by changing beliefs I didn't realize I was holding. You'll discover a powerful method that has helped couples heal from betrayal, parents reconnect with their children, and leaders rebuild trust across teams and organizations.

You'll see why the thing likely holding your closest relationships back isn't the other person, but rather the beliefs you've never thought to question.

FROM LIMITING BELIEFS...	TO LIBERATING BELIEFS...
What you see is all there is. I see reality accurately.	I'm seeing my own personal version of reality.
My first impression is usually correct.	Perception is data, not truth—I can question my initial interpretation.
"I'm not good at this."	Talk about yourself in the third person: "Sarah is struggling with this at the moment but will figure it out soon."
I should focus on what confirms my existing beliefs.	I can actively seek evidence that contradicts my assumptions.
I need to see it to believe it.	Beliefs change what I'm able to see.
Analyzing my problems repeatedly helps me solve them.	Not every thought loop is progress—I'll notice when it's rumination, not problem-solving.

CHAPTER 3

The Secret to Better Relationships

You don't have relationship problems. You have perception problems.

"WELL, OK, I'LL be sure never to send you flowers again."

The sarcastic words hung in the air as the video call grew awkwardly silent. In that moment, I could almost see myself from above—a forty-five-year-old published author with my own family—suddenly transformed into an insecure teenager, complete with eye rolls and dramatic sighs.

It had started innocently enough. Even though I was living in Singapore, I'd gone to considerable trouble to find a local florist in Central Florida, wanting to surprise my mom with flowers for her seventy-fourth. When I called to wish her happy birthday, she thanked me but then added, "You may want to call the shop. The flowers they sent are already half-dying. Or maybe don't order from them."

In an instant, I felt a familiar sting of rejection wash over me. My inner monologue erupted: Instead of appreciating the gesture, she was criticizing my effort. Why do I even bother? She's so hard to please.

I felt my jaw tighten, my chest constrict, and that unmistakable flush of indignation spread across my face. Three decades of adult development, professional accomplishments, and personal growth had evaporated in seconds, all over a well-intentioned birthday gift.

Our closest relationships are deeply personal and unique to us, but the challenges they pose are universal. Most of us have experienced how certain people seem to flip an internal switch in us, activating automatic responses that bypass our conscious control. Around parents, we become children again. With former classmates, we revert to old social roles. With certain authority figures, we transform into anxious, approval-seeking versions of ourselves.

This brings us to the heart of the First Power of Belief. Throughout the last two chapters, we've seen that what we believe determines what we see. We've tracked how our beliefs create perceptual filters that shape our experience of reality. Nowhere is this power more evident—or more consequential—than in our relationships with others.

The beliefs we hold about our parents, partners, friends, and colleagues determine what we're capable of seeing in them. For decades, I viewed my mother through the lens of "too critical and hard to please"—a belief that turned her comments into personal attacks. If we want to change our relationships, the best place to start is with the underlying beliefs that shape our perception of others.

The Pitfalls of Venting

After the Zoom call ended, my wife turned to me with a gentle expression. "Would you like my help doing The Work on this, or do you need to sit with it for a bit?" In that moment, I blinked at her, momentarily speechless. I didn't want to engage in any self-help mumbo jumbo; I wanted to vent—to have my feelings validated. I wanted to build a case for why I was the reasonable party and my mother was at fault.

Venting my frustrations felt natural and right, even justified. After all, isn't that what we're supposed to do with difficult emotions: express them, get them out, release the pressure?

But research tells a startlingly different story. Expressing anger doesn't reduce it; it amplifies it. Venting our negative beliefs about others only reinforces them, locking us into poisonous relationship dynamics that make us feel worse instead of better.[1]

My wife was inviting me to shift my perception of my mother. But the very idea of changing the way you see someone who's close to you can be daunting. In some cases, we're talking about changing our perceptions of people we've known our whole lives. For better or worse, these close relationships make up the fabric of our reality. Questioning those basic assumptions can be scary. It certainly was for me.

At the same time, some exceptionally wise thinkers have taught us that living a full life requires questioning what we think we know. Over 2,400 years ago, Socrates roamed the streets of Athens, engaging citizens in dialogues that systematically examined their most deeply held assumptions. His method wasn't to impose his views but to ask probing questions that revealed contradictions in their thinking.

Eastern philosophical traditions developed similar approaches. Buddhist teachings emphasize the importance of perceiving reality without the distortions of attachment, aversion, and ignorance. The concept of *anattā* (non-self) challenges the fixed belief in a permanent, unchanging self—a belief that often underlies our most reactive patterns in relationships.

Notably, while these insights originated in philosophical and spiritual traditions, their application requires no supernatural beliefs or religious affiliation. They represent practical, empirical approaches to perception.

In the twentieth century, these ancient insights found expression in new forms, like cognitive therapy, which identified systematic errors in thinking that contributed to mental health issues, and rational emotive behavior therapy (REBT), which helped people identify and dispute the "irrational beliefs" underlying their emotional disturbances.[2]

In the 1970s, authors like Ken Keyes Jr. brought these insights to a broader audience through books like *Handbook to Higher Consciousness*,[3] which taught readers to recognize beliefs that created unnecessary suffering.

These approaches share a basic recognition: The way we see others can look like rock-solid reality, but in fact, our perceptions are profoundly shaped by our beliefs. By developing greater flexibility in these areas, we can expand our perceptual range and choose from a wider portfolio of perspectives in any given relationship.

The Judgment Trap

But how can we change our deeply held beliefs about others? To reshape our beliefs, we first need to recognize the judgment trap: a perceptual pattern that operates automatically and largely unconsciously in our relationships.

In my case, when my mother commented on the wilting flowers,

I immediately jumped to a specific interpretation: "She's criticizing me instead of appreciating my gift."

This judgment felt true. But was it? Could there be other ways to understand her comment?

Once I formed the belief that my mother was being critical and unappreciative, my attention automatically filtered for evidence that confirmed this view. I noticed her tone of voice, remembered past instances when I felt criticized, and completely missed the appreciation she had expressed at the beginning of the call. My belief that I was being criticized determined what I was capable of perceiving.

Researcher Ellen Langer refers to this as a form of "mindlessness" that often creeps into long-term relationships.[4] Once we think we know someone, we stop truly seeing them. We interact with our mental image of them rather than the actual person standing before us. The longer we've known them, the more certain we feel in our assumptions of who they "are" and, paradoxically, the less accurately we see them.

In the previous chapter, we learned how researchers manipulated study participants into perceiving neutral faces as threatening by showing them fewer threatening faces.[5] When people looked for something that wasn't there, they created it in their minds. Unfortunately, the same happens in our relationships.

Once we start looking for evidence that someone is inconsiderate, uncaring, or disrespectful, we'll continue to find it—even if the actual inconsiderate behavior decreases. To maintain our belief, our criterion for what counts as "uncaring" continues to expand. A "good morning" that isn't enthusiastic enough gets interpreted as a rude insult.

This judgment trap creates a self-fulfilling prophecy. As psychologist Sandra Murray found in a study that tracked couples over three weeks, people who felt well-regarded by their partners found it easier to brush off small slights. However, those who felt less appreciated tended to read more into stressful events.[6] Our beliefs shape what we see, which influences how we act, and this in turn affects how others respond, ultimately confirming our initial belief.

I experienced this cycle myself in my relationship with my mother. I already believed she was overly critical and hard to please, which made me notice every instance of perceived criticism while filtering out her words of appreciation. This led me to respond defensively, which made her feel that I was being short with her. She reacted harshly, which I then interpreted as evidence that she was impossible to please. The cycle continued, reinforcing my belief that *she* was the problem.

My wife, witnessing the same interaction, wasn't caught in this trap. Without the same belief filters, she heard my mother's comment about the flowers simply as practical information, not as criticism or rejection: same words, completely different perception. This difference wasn't about who was right or wrong. It was about how our beliefs shape what we're capable of seeing.

Questioning Beliefs

When my wife suggested "doing The Work" on my reaction to my mother, she was referring to the structured practice developed by author Byron Katie. I knew from witnessing my wife's experience that The Work had transformed her relationship with her own mother, even though her mother hadn't changed at all. My wife was noticeably calmer around her parents; she seemed happier, and the change had even flowed into our marriage. Persistent problems we'd had in the past seemed to resolve, and we felt closer than ever before.

Reluctantly, I followed my wife's suggestion. I took out a piece of paper and a pen, and thought back to the specific situation. I started by identifying the belief that was causing my suffering: "My mother is too critical and hard to please."

From there, Katie's four questions guided my inquiry, which I've adapted below.[7]

1. **Is this belief true?**

    Yes! Of course it's true. What else could it be? What my mother had said was definitely criticism, plain and simple. If flowers sent from around the world couldn't please a mother, well then, nothing could. She *was* too hard to please.

2. **Can I be certain this belief is true?**

    At first I thought, "Isn't this just the same question?" However, as I considered it, I realized I needed to examine what had actually happened. She had thanked me for the flowers and then added information about their condition. Was that necessarily a criticism of me, or was I assuming it was?

    This deeper question pushed me further. When I genuinely considered it, I had to acknowledge that I couldn't be absolutely, 100 percent certain that her comment about the wilting flowers was criticism. I couldn't know her intention or what she was thinking when she made the comment. Perhaps she was simply letting me know in case I wanted to contact the florist, as she suggested.

This simple recognition—that my interpretation contained even a bit of uncertainty—created the first crack in my belief. I felt a subtle loosening in my chest, as though something tightly wound had been given just enough space to breathe.

3. **How do I react when I believe this?**

   This question helped me recognize the real-world consequences of my belief about my mother. I saw that when I believed "My mother is too critical and hard to please," I immediately felt hurt and defensive. I responded sarcastically with a hurtful comment: "Well, OK, I'll be sure to never send you flowers again." I transformed a potentially neutral exchange into a conflict, ruining what could have been a pleasant birthday call.

   I realized this was a familiar pattern—how many holiday calls, visits, and special occasions had been tainted by my instant interpretation of her comments as criticism? Each of those times, my belief about my mother's words had shaped my perception of her actions. Caught up in my own interpretation, I failed to hear what she was actually saying.

   Most importantly, I realized it wasn't the comment that was causing me pain; it was my belief about what it meant. The overthinking, the ruminating, the anger I kept replaying: They were all happening in my own head. And none of them were necessary.

4. **Who would I be without this belief?**

   This powerful question invited me to imagine how I might experience the same situation differently, without my interpretation. Without the belief that "My mother is too critical and hard to please," I might have interpreted her comment more neutrally. I might have responded with, "Oh, that's disappointing," or "Thanks for letting me know." Without this belief, I would have stayed present in the birthday call, focusing on connection rather than perceived criticism. I might have asked about her plans for the day or shared other birthday wishes without a cloud of defensiveness coloring our interaction.

These four questions didn't lead me to a forced positive conclusion about my mother's comment. They created space between my automatic interpretation and what was actually said. In that space, I could finally acknowledge that my automatic interpretation was hurting me more than her comment had. This opened a door to different perspectives that might be equally, or possibly more, true.

The Turnaround

After questioning my belief about my mother through these four questions, I moved on to the next step: deliberately exploring those alternatives. Katie calls this part of the process "the turnaround." It involves purposefully experimenting with alternative ways to view a challenging situation.

The belief I started with was "My mother is too critical and hard to please." Katie proposes three different ways of turning around a belief like this. She calls them the Turnarounds to the Opposite, to the Other, and to the Self, and they each ask us to reframe the belief in question in a different way.

Let's look at them in turn.

1. **Turnaround to the Opposite**

   "My mother is too critical and hard to please." → "My mother is not too critical and hard to please."

   Initially, this seemed obviously false. However, when I genuinely sought evidence in this specific situation, I found more than I had expected. My mother had, after all, thanked me for the flowers at the beginning of our call. She hadn't criticized me personally or suggested I had done something wrong. She had provided information about the state of the flowers and offered a practical suggestion about contacting the florist. Was that actually criticism, or was I interpreting it as criticism because of my longstanding belief?

   After further consideration, I acknowledged that her suggestion to check with the florist or choose a different one next time was quite reasonable. If I had paid for flowers that arrived wilted, I would want to know. Perhaps she was trying to be helpful rather than critical.

2. **Turnaround to the Other**

   "My mother is too critical and hard to please." → "I am too critical and hard to please toward my mother."

   This turnaround revealed an unexpected truth about this situation. I realized I was being extremely critical of my mother's response to my gift. I wanted not just thanks but a specific kind of effusive gratitude. When she didn't respond exactly as I wanted, I immediately judged her as critical and dismissed her actual thanks. In that moment, I was the one being hard to please, demanding that she express appreciation in precisely the way I expected.

I saw how I was imposing impossible standards on her communication. I was scrutinizing her words, tone, and timing, looking for the slightest hint of criticism. Even when she expressed a straightforward fact, I was quick to interpret it in a negative light. *I* was virtually impossible to please in how *I* wanted her to communicate with me.

3. Turnaround to the Self

"My mother is too critical and hard to please." → "I am too critical and hard to please toward myself."

This final turnaround offered yet another perspective—the hardest to see and ultimately the most true. I realized how harshly I judged myself in this situation. I had immediately taken her comment about the flowers as a reflection on me, as though I had failed in some way by choosing the wrong florist. My self-criticism was so ready to activate that even a simple comment about wilting flowers became evidence of my inadequacy.

I saw how I set impossible standards for myself as a son. I believed I should somehow know exactly which florist would deliver perfect flowers, and that anything less than perfection was a failure. I was harder on myself than anyone else could be, creating a situation where I was constantly falling short of my own impossible expectations.

By turning around my judgment in these three ways, I didn't arrive at a single "correct" interpretation to replace my original belief. Instead, I developed a broader range of possible ways to view the same interaction. This expanded perceptual range gave me more freedom to choose what I wanted to believe and how I might respond next time.

And with more practice, I might be less likely to lock onto the first negative interpretation that surfaced.

Most strikingly, I noticed how my body felt different as I considered these turnarounds. The tightness in my chest loosened. My breathing deepened. The defensive tension in my shoulders relaxed. This physical shift suggested I was touching something true, even if it contradicted my initial certainty.

A Portfolio of Perspectives

What makes the turnaround approach so powerful is that it doesn't just replace one rigid belief with another. Instead, it helps us develop what I call a *portfolio of perspectives*—a range of possible ways to view the same relationship or situation.

Consider Caleb, my friend who did The Work during a difficult time with his girlfriend. Caleb described feeling deeply hurt when he wasn't invited to a concert his girlfriend was going to with a group of mutual friends. His immediate interpretation was "She doesn't want me at the concert" and, more deeply, "She doesn't really love me"—beliefs that triggered feelings of rejection and inadequacy. By asking himself the four questions, Caleb was able to turn these beliefs around to discover several alternative perspectives:

- "She does want me at the concert." Caleb realized the concert tickets weren't his girlfriend's to give. She'd been invited by one of her friends.
- "I don't want me at the concert." Caleb actually felt grateful for not having to go, admitting, "I don't even like the band" and "I hate being around lots of drunk people acting stupid."

- "I don't really love myself." Caleb began to see how his insecurities were coloring his perception. He realized he just wanted his girlfriend to want him. The concert wasn't the real issue.

Is the idea to look through these alternatives to replace the original belief with a "correct" new one? No. The goal is to assemble a portfolio of perspectives, each with some truth to it. That portfolio gave Caleb the freedom to choose the perspective that served him best in any given moment, and it helped him feel less attached to a single, painful view.

It's crucial to keep in mind that this method is very different from "positive thinking" approaches that aim to replace "negative" thoughts with "positive" ones without questioning either. (We'll explore more of the pitfalls of positive thinking in a later chapter.) It also differs from conventional advice to "communicate better," which assumes that the problem lies in expression rather than perception.

Instead, the turnaround method helps us see that our perceptions themselves are choices, and by expanding the portfolio of perspectives available to us, we gain freedom in how we relate to others.

In cognitive behavioral therapy, therapists use a similar concept called *cognitive flexibility*, which is the ability to adapt one's thinking to changing situations rather than remaining rigidly attached to a single interpretation. Research shows that greater cognitive flexibility is associated with more resilient personal relationships.[8]

Whether we call it a portfolio of perspectives, the turnaround method, or cognitive flexibility, the key insight is the same: Harmony in relationships doesn't come from finding the one "true" way to see others. It stems from developing the capacity to shift perspectives, allowing us to choose to see what best serves connection and understanding at any given moment.

Over time, as I continued to question my beliefs about my mom, our relationship gradually shifted from one characterized by mutual defensiveness to one of genuine appreciation and understanding. I began to see qualities in her that I had been filtering out for years—her practicality, her subtle humor, her unwavering support—even when expressed in ways I hadn't recognized.

Most importantly, I stopped being seized by teenage reactions during our interactions. I could remain present as my adult self, responding to what was happening, rather than to the stories I had accumulated over the decades. This shift didn't require her to change at all—it came entirely from changing my own beliefs.

The Science of Perspective Shifts

While the practice of turning around beliefs has deep historical roots, scientific research on its effects is still emerging.

Studies show that Byron Katie's method (formally called *inquiry-based stress reduction*) improves psychological well-being, self-acceptance, and relationship quality while reducing emotional exhaustion.[9] Research on cognitive reappraisal—consciously changing one's interpretation of situations—reveals that it reduces activity in emotional centers such as the amygdala while increasing activity in the prefrontal cortex, resulting in improved emotional regulation and better relationship outcomes over time.[10]

But perhaps the most powerful explanation for how turnarounds work lies in their ability to interrupt our confirmation bias. By deliberately looking for evidence that contradicts our judgments, the turnaround creates a kind of *disconfirmation* effect that counteracts our natural tendency toward selective perception.[11] This explains why people who practice turnarounds often report seeing sides of others they never noticed before: Their attention is finally directed toward evidence they had been filtering out.

These findings align with what practitioners have observed for years: Changing how we think about others changes how we see them, how we behave toward them, and ultimately the quality of our relationships with them.

Like most profound insights, the turnaround method is simple to understand but challenging to apply, especially in moments of intense emotion. Here are some practical ways to integrate it into your relationships.

START WITH SMALL IRRITATIONS

Before tackling your most painful relationship judgments, practice with minor annoyances: the person who cuts you off in traffic, the barista who gets your order wrong, the family member with irritating habits. These situations provide low-stakes opportunities to practice questioning your immediate interpretations.

In my own life, I began with minor irritations over my teenage daughter's behavior. These moments became my training ground before I tackled the deeper judgments about my mother that had accumulated over the course of decades. When my daughter responded to a request with a tone I didn't like, the emotional charge was strong enough to notice, but not so overwhelming that I couldn't step back and question my interpretation. Was she really being disrespectful, or was I reading into something that wasn't there? Was I seeing her clearly, or was I filtering her behavior through my expectations?

The karmic irony wasn't lost on me: I had to work through judgments about my daughter to heal my relationship with my mother. The pattern-breaking felt almost miraculous. As I learned to question my rigid beliefs about each of them, my connections with these important women in my life transformed from tension-filled encounters I dreaded into relationships I cherished. Where once I saw only criticism and resistance, I began discovering thoughtfulness and love that had been there all along, waiting for me to notice.

CREATE A JUDGMENT JOURNAL

Set aside time to write down your strongest judgments from the day. Choose one to turn around, finding at least three genuine examples of beliefs that are as true as, if not more true than, the belief you're challenging. This regular practice builds the mental muscle of questioning your certainty.

A friend of mine discovered that simply writing down her judgments—"My husband never helps with the kids," "My boss doesn't respect my time"—created an immediate shift in perspective. Seeing these absolute statements on paper made their exaggeration more obvious, helping her find exceptions and alternative viewpoints.

INSTALL A JUDGMENT ALERT

Certain phrases signal unquestioned judgments: "always," "never," "every time," "just like them," "typical." When you catch yourself using these kinds of terms, take it as a cue to pause and question whether you're seeing the whole picture.

I've installed a mental alarm that goes off whenever I think "That's so like her" about my mother. This phrase usually signals that I'm in my judgment trap, seeing her through my filters rather than with fresh eyes.

SEEK THE GRAIN OF TRUTH

Instead of dismissing the turnaround belief as obviously false, look for the smallest way it might be true. Does it have even a 2 percent chance of being true? Even a sliver of a truth can open your perception to information you've been filtering out.

When I initially tried to turn my belief from "My mother is too critical and hard to please" into "My mother is not too critical and hard to please," I resisted. However, when I genuinely sought examples, I found many ways I had failed to acknowledge times when she showed support and was not at all hard to please, like waking up for 7 a.m. video calls to connect across continents.

PRACTICE EMPATHIC REFLECTION

Before expressing frustration about someone's behavior, try to imagine at least three plausible explanations for it that don't involve negative intentions. This quick practice interrupts automatic negative attributions.

On another occasion, when my mother made a comment about my parenting that I initially perceived as criticism, I paused and considered: Maybe she's sharing what worked for her. Maybe she's expressing concern because she cares. Perhaps she's simply making conversation about a topic that connects us. This brief reflection completely changed how I responded.

LISTEN FOR DEFENSIVENESS

Your strongest resistance to a turnaround often signals where it has the most to teach you. When you find yourself thinking, "That's definitely not true," explore that resistance with particular curiosity.

My strongest resistance came with the turnaround "I am too critical and hard to please." I initially rejected this completely—wasn't *she* the critical one? But this resistance pointed directly to the truth I needed most: I was indeed constantly criticizing her in my mind, creating a dynamic of mutual criticism that kept us locked in conflict.

The turnaround practice isn't suitable for everyone in every situation. Those in acute crisis, severe mental illness, or early grief may require different approaches initially. This work demands a certain psychological readiness and should be approached with discernment and care. The goal is to liberate ourselves from perceptual limitations that cause unnecessary suffering, not to deny legitimate problems that necessitate action.

The Ultimate Turnaround

While most turnarounds focus on our judgments about specific others, the method eventually leads to what might be called the ultimate turnaround—the recognition that our judgments about others are, in fact, judgments about ourselves.

This isn't just true in the obvious sense of projection, where we criticize in others what we dislike in ourselves (though that often happens). Our judgments reveal our values, fears, unmet needs, and interpretive frameworks. In the end, they tell us more about how we see the world than about the people we're judging.

Consider a simple example: Two colleagues observe the same co-worker arriving late to a meeting. One thinks, "How disrespectful! She clearly doesn't value our time." The other thinks, "She must be having a rough morning. I hope everything's okay." Same behavior, radically different interpretations. Each response reveals something about the observer: their values, assumptions, and sensitivities.

Our judgments are like mirrors, reflecting back our inner landscape. When I react strongly to what feels like criticism from my mother, it's often because her words touch something important to me: my value for appreciation, my fear of disapproval, and my need for validation. My wife, witnessing the same behavior, doesn't have the same reaction. She's not carrying the same values, fears, and needs to the interaction.

This insight can transform our perspective on conflict. If our judgments are ultimately about us, then relationship difficulties become invitations to self-understanding rather than battles to win. When my mother's behavior sets me off, the turnaround invites me to ask: What does my reaction reveal about me? What values, fears, or needs are being activated?

This ultimate turnaround leads to a profound shift in how we view relationships. Instead of focusing on how others should change to meet our needs, we start with our own role. This doesn't mean we stop setting boundaries or expressing preferences; it means we do so from a place of clarity and self-responsibility, rather than blame or demand.

This practice doesn't ask us to deny facts or excuse harmful behavior. It invites us to question the beliefs behind our reactions, broadening our awareness of reality. When our perception expands in that way, we don't passively accept mistreatment; we become better equipped to formulate clearer, more effective responses to what is happening.

My journey with this practice has led me to a startling conclusion: *The quality of my relationships depends far more on my beliefs than on others' behavior.*

When I change what I believe about someone, I literally change what I'm capable of seeing in them. And when I see them differently, I act differently toward them, which often transforms how they respond to me. By taking responsibility for our beliefs and our attention, we reclaim our power to transform our relationships without waiting for others to change.

Whether we're dealing with minor irritations, such as a perceived criticism from a parent, or major challenges like betrayal or abuse, the turnaround offers a path to freedom by addressing the root cause of much relationship suffering: the unquestioned belief in thoughts that aren't true. By questioning these beliefs and considering their opposites, we expand our perception beyond the narrow confines of judgment, allowing us to see more of what's really there.

In the next chapter, we'll see why the First Power of Belief is the foundation for business and financial success. You're about to meet an ambitious young woman who literally helped tens of thousands of unhoused people get back on their feet. Then you'll be amazed by how that same woman leveraged her beliefs to build a fitness empire worth hundreds of millions of dollars.

You'll learn specific techniques for spotting opportunities that others miss by training yourself to create your own luck. By understanding how to direct your attention using the First Power of Belief, you'll be able to see opportunities where others see impossibilities. This capacity to look beyond conventional wisdom to spot enriching possibilities before they're obvious is what separates visionary entrepreneurs from those who follow well-worn paths.

Whether you dream of building your own business or simply providing enough for your family's future, you'll learn why beliefs make all the difference.

FROM LIMITING BELIEFS...	TO LIBERATING BELIEFS...
They need to change for this relationship to improve.	My beliefs shape my experience of this relationship.
They always act this way. This is just how they are.	I'm interacting with my mental image of them, not who they actually are.
That comment clearly means they don't care about me or my feelings.	I can't absolutely know their intention—I'm interpreting their words through my own lens, not reading their mind.
If I feel hurt, someone else must be at fault.	My reaction reveals my own values, fears, and unmet needs.
Venting makes me feel better.	Venting actually reinforces my beliefs. Questioning my beliefs creates real relief.
They're trying to hurt or criticize me.	Their behavior might be practical information, not a personal attack.
I can't help how I react to them.	I can pause and ask: "Is this interpretation serving me? Is it absolutely true?"

CHAPTER 4

How to See Opportunities Others Miss

Luck isn't chance.

O N A PHILADELPHIA street corner at 5:30 a.m., a twentysomething jogger ran past the same homeless men she'd seen hundreds of times before. They were always there, clustered outside the Sunday Breakfast Rescue Mission in the pre-dawn darkness. Like most city dwellers, Anne Mahlum had mastered the art of practiced indifference—averting her eyes, maintaining her pace, treating their presence as just another fixture of the urban landscape.

But one morning, one of them waved. She waved back.

The next day, one of the men sent a sarcastic joke her way. "They would ask me if all I do is run all day," Mahlum recalls, "and I would ask them if all they do there is stand all day."[1] Just a flicker of connection, but she later described it as the beginning of an "amazing rapport" built on playful verbal sparring.

These casual interactions sparked a question that stopped her mid-stride during a run: "Why do I get to be the runner, and these guys get to be the homeless guys on the corner? Why can't we all be runners?"[2]

She didn't have an answer. It would've been easy to let that question dissolve with her footsteps, to continue running past the men she admitted she previously "didn't give a damn about." Most people would have. But Mahlum saw something in those men that others had missed: potential.

Ten years later, this same ability to see what others couldn't would earn Mahlum nearly $100 million when she sold [solidcore], the fitness empire she built from a cramped basement studio in Washington, DC.

When reporters ask her if she had ever imagined such success, Mahlum answers without hesitation. "Who do you think's been driving the bus? Of course I did! I know exactly how I got here."[3]

That kind of certainty wasn't born overnight. It came from a core belief Mahlum had cultivated for years: that people could transform in ways others thought impossible. She had learned to see opportunities where others saw nothing. And it all started with witnessing an unlikely comeback much closer to home.

The First Turnaround

Long before Mahlum ran a company, she ran circles around her neighborhood in Bismarck, North Dakota. At twelve, she was wound tight as a spring, and desperately trying to outpace the chaos waiting at home.

Mahlum's father had gambled away $50,000 that the family didn't have. For her mother, a frugal schoolteacher who tracked every penny, it was an insurmountable betrayal. The marriage collapsed. "I just felt really inadequate," Mahlum said, her voice softening with the memory. "In my small town, people knew my business. Everybody knew that my dad was a gambling addict and my parents didn't live together."[4]

She kept running. At first, it was pure escape. Over time, it became something more profound: a ritual of structure and self-definition. "Running was therapeutic for me," Mahlum explained. "It helped me through depression, anxiety, and sadness. It gives you this sense of confidence and accomplishment before most people even wake up."

What happened next would reshape everything Mahlum believed about human potential. Her father—the man who had lost everything, who had been kicked out of his home, who seemed beyond redemption—began to change. Slowly, painstakingly, he rebuilt his life. He got help. He controlled his gambling. The marriage didn't survive, but he did.

Watching her father's transformation planted a seed in Mahlum's mind that would define her worldview. She didn't just believe in hard work—she believed in second acts. In comebacks. In the possibility that anyone, no matter how far they'd fallen, could rebuild if they had structure, support, and someone beside them who refused to abandon hope.

That belief became an internal compass. It shaped what she noticed, what she remembered, and what she interpreted as progress versus failure. At the time, she wouldn't have called it a "perceptual filter." But that's precisely what it was.

That's why, years later, when that invisible man outside the homeless shelter waved, she saw him in a way no one else did and waved back.

Back on My Feet

The first time Mahlum invited the men from the shelter to join her for a morning run, nine showed up. Most of them were skeptical; a few were still half asleep. She had no program. No degree in social work. Just an unshakable belief that perhaps running could do for them what it had once done for her.

Then something extraordinary happened. "Over the course of a few weeks, I began to see these guys light up about what they were doing and who they were becoming." Her voice quickens with the memory. "You think about homelessness and the stereotypes that surround it, right? You're lazy, you're probably a drug addict ... dangerous, you don't have any drive. And then you think [about] somebody who runs three days a week at six in the morning—that person is disciplined, focused, reliable, responsible, ambitious."

Mahlum had trained herself to look for what she believed in. Where others saw setbacks, she spotted breakthroughs. A man showing up on time. Another man running an extra city block when he could have stopped. A story of vulnerability shared during their post-run huddle. These were signals, each one a confirmation of what she already believed. These men were capable of rebuilding their lives.

The more Mahlum believed in their potential, the more she noticed evidence of it. The more she observed, the deeper her belief grew. Simultaneously, the men began to see themselves differently as well. Each mile logged was a vote of confidence in a new identity. "When we tell people they're capable, they start to believe it too," Mahlum says.[5]

That small circle of runners became the foundation for a nonprofit called Back on My Feet. The idea was simple: Invite people experiencing homelessness to run with volunteers three mornings a week. From there, offer pathways such as job training, financial literacy, and housing support.

Mahlum was acutely aware that a running program wouldn't solve all the systemic causes of homelessness. Affordable housing shortages, mental health care gaps, substance abuse issues, and economic inequalities couldn't be fixed with running shoes. But she wasn't trying to solve homelessness as a societal problem; she was focused on helping the individuals right in front of her find a path forward.

Of course, not every mile was easy. She admits there were "stories you wouldn't believe." Some of the men took her car for a joyride and returned it littered with empty beer cans. Others stole from the organization. One, she said, had to be sent to jail because, in her words, "it was the best place for him."

None of it changed her fundamental conviction. Mahlum had already rewired how she saw these men. She processed the theft, the betrayals, and the men who weren't ready as temporary setbacks rather than proof of failure. She wasn't ignoring reality or being blindly optimistic. She simply chose to focus on possibilities rather than problems.

Just seven years after its founding, Back on My Feet had grown into a national movement. Sixteen chapters. More than fifteen thousand people served. Over ten thousand jobs and housing placements. Nearly one million miles run.[6]

Entrepreneurial Alertness

Mahlum's transformation from a runner who ignored homeless men to someone who saw untapped potential in them wasn't random. It was the result of a specific type of perceptual training. Psychologists refer to this as *belief-consistent information processing*—the tendency to seek out, remember, and emphasize information that confirms our existing beliefs while unconsciously filtering out contradictory evidence.

Remember the checkerboard illusion from chapter 2? Your brain insists that squares A and B are different colors, even when you know they're identical. Mahlum experienced something similar, but in reverse. Where most people's brains automatically filtered out the men outside the shelter—seeing them as hopeless cases or "not my problem"—Mahlum's beliefs had rewired her attention to see something different.

This shift began with her father's recovery. Watching someone rebuild from a gambling addiction had instilled a belief in Mahlum that transformation was possible. That belief changed what her brain flagged as important, focusing her attention on new possibilities others couldn't see.

When one of the homeless men waved at her, she noticed it and returned the greeting. When they joked about her constant running, she didn't hear mockery—she heard an invitation for connection. The same resilience she'd witnessed in her father's recovery suddenly became visible in these interactions. Her perceptual filter made those moments matter.

Mahlum wasn't consciously scanning for nonprofit opportunities. But her beliefs had created what psychologists call *entrepreneurial alertness*—a heightened sensitivity to patterns others miss.[7] Her mind was already calibrated to recognize the signs of potential transformation: discipline, humor under pressure, and showing up despite difficult circumstances.

This is how beliefs create visionary entrepreneurs. Beliefs don't just change what you think is possible; they change what you're capable of seeing as possible. Here was the First Power of Belief in action. What you believe shapes what you see. And what you see shapes what you do.

Making Your Own Luck

Mahlum's early experience founding Back on My Feet is an example of *provoked luck*—when small actions create big opportunities that, in hindsight, seem like simple good fortune. Researchers now know that more often than not, luck isn't chance.

Dr. Richard Wiseman spent over a decade studying why some people feel perpetually "lucky" while others always feel "unlucky." His research revealed that so-called lucky individuals don't actually experience more good fortune; they simply see more of it.

In one of Wiseman's most famous studies, he asked participants to flip through a newspaper and count the number of photos it contained. What they didn't know was that halfway through, a huge ad proclaimed:

"Stop counting. There are 43 photos in this newspaper."

Below this was a second message:

"Tell the experimenter you have seen this and win $250."

Most "unlucky" participants missed the message entirely. They were so focused on completing the assigned task that they filtered out everything else—including a cash prize staring them in the face. Meanwhile, those who considered themselves lucky were far more likely to spot the message and claim the money.[8] The winners weren't imagining their luck. They were looking wider and seeing more.

As the scientist Louis Pasteur famously observed, "Chance favors the prepared mind."[9] Anne Mahlum's mind was prepared by years of belief-building. But how exactly do you build a "lucky" mindset? Research points to specific practices anyone can adopt.

PUSH PAST YOUR COMFORT ZONE

Lucky people consistently disrupt their routines. Dr. Tina Seelig at Stanford University has her students fill out a "risk-o-meter" to identify their comfort zones, then deliberately step outside them. It could be as simple as taking a different route to work, striking up a conversation with a stranger, or volunteering for a project outside your expertise.[10]

Seelig has her own story of how risk-taking led to luck. She started a conversation with a stranger on a plane who turned out to be a publisher. During the flight, she pitched him a book proposal that he rejected on the spot. But Seelig continued to nurture the relationship with him. She invited him to speak to her college class on the future of publishing and sent him videos of her students' projects. Eventually, she sold that same book proposal to an editor who was a coworker of that publisher.

SHOW APPRECIATION

According to Seelig, everyone who helps you on your journey plays a crucial role in helping you achieve your goals. Failing to show appreciation is a missed opportunity. At the end of every day, she reviews her calendar and sends brief thank-you messages to people she has interacted with. This practice pays, she says.

Seelig once received a thank-you from a student who had been rejected twice from an entrepreneurial fellowship Seelig oversaw. The student thanked her for the opportunity and said he had learned a great deal through the application process. The note moved Seelig so much that she invited the student to chat over coffee and ultimately decided to advise him on an independent study project that he later turned into a business.

SET "FAILURE GOALS"

Dr. Joël Le Bon at Johns Hopkins University suggests, counterintuitively, setting targets for rejection, not just success. Aim for fifty noes this month. Get turned down by ten dream clients. This reframes failure from something to avoid into something to collect—and paradoxically increases your chances of success.

Mahlum's early attempts at helping the homeless men were marked by numerous setbacks. Some stole from the organization. Others relapsed into substance abuse. But she had already reframed these moments: They weren't failures; they were data points on the path to figuring out what worked.

Researchers have found that "provoked luck" accounts for the majority of breakthrough moments. In one study of salespeople,[11] approximately 60 percent of total sales resulted from lucky circumstances. However, between 76 percent and 88 percent of those "lucky" sales were actually the outcomes of strategic actions that created the conditions for luck to occur.

Mahlum didn't stumble into her moment of insight outside that homeless shelter. Years of believing had prepared her to see it. Years of pushing past comfort zones had forged her willingness to act. Years of turning setbacks into stepping stones had given her the resilience to build on that willingness. She didn't just get lucky. She engineered the conditions for luck to find her. And it was about to find her once again.

The Pink Studio

As Back on My Feet expanded into new cities, Mahlum found herself in constant motion. While visiting Los Angeles to launch a new chapter, she noticed a bright, pink fitness studio, "very LA and very cute" as she later described it.[12] Curious, she stepped inside.

The branding was bold, the energy electric, and the workout absolutely brutal. "I got my butt kicked," she later said, laughing. "I couldn't believe how hard it was." She wasn't there to start a business, but her mind was already trained to scan for transformation in all its forms. This place radiated opportunity—small, yes, but brimming with untapped potential.

She began dissecting the studio's business model like a forensic accountant. She examined the pricing structure, operational efficiency, brand positioning, and scalability. It was a gold mine hiding in plain sight. Mahlum had witnessed firsthand how shared movement could reshape self-perception. Back on My Feet had proven that. But now, she was thinking about a different audience—people searching for their own version of forward momentum, ready to invest in a framework for change.

She decided to bet nearly everything she had on herself and a new company. Rather than taking outside investment, even from a trusted mentor, Mahlum put $175,000 of her savings on the line to launch her first fitness studio. She leased a space so small that clients could barely move between the equipment.[13] The aesthetic was deliberately raw: exposed concrete walls, industrial fixtures, and harsh lighting.[14] No amenities. No juice bar. No showers.

The name—[solidcore]—came wrapped in brackets like a vise, signaling everything held tight: tight muscles, a tight community, and yes, tight bodies emerging from the workout. Mahlum had the two brackets tattooed on her ribs.

Mahlum always believed she'd "build an empire." The day she opened her first studio, she wrote down her ambition using those very words. Below her plan to "open 100 locations and then I'm going to sell the company," she wrote, "I can do this. I know I can do this."[15]

Within two years, [solidcore] was a phenomenon. Studios opened across the country. Revenue soared. Mahlum was earning seven figures and gaining recognition as a fitness visionary. The same belief that once saw possibility in a group of men outside a homeless shelter was now helping thousands of people reshape their bodies and their lives.

In just a few short years, Mahlum had built two movements from the ground up, powered by her beliefs. But there was an unanticipated price to her convictions.

The Belief Blind Spot

Each success seemed to reinforce what Mahlum believed about herself: Her vision was crystal clear. Her judgment was sound. Her approach worked.

However, the same filters that help us see what's possible can also conceal things we'd rather not see. When conviction becomes an integral part of your identity, it becomes increasingly difficult to accept feedback. The very beliefs that fueled your rise can become the ones that hinder your growth.

It was easy to rationalize away the early warning signs. When a few longtime team members at Back on My Feet stepped away, Mahlum's instinct was to double down. "You can't build a movement nine to five,"[16] she told her team. "This is an everyday thing—all the time." In many ways, she was right. Movements do demand sustained energy. But belief without reflection has a tendency to calcify. What begins as clarity can harden into rigidity.

Her intensity was everywhere at [solidcore]: on the walls, in the workouts, in the culture itself. In the early years, that energy was rocket fuel. Mahlum's belief in what the brand could become gave the team a clear target. The standards were sky-high, but the results spoke for themselves. Still, a familiar tension was building beneath the surface.

Mahlum's passion often erupted in harsh critiques and public callouts. When she sensed someone wasn't matching her pace, she could grow impatient, even volatile.

While some employees described Mahlum as passionate, others saw a different version entirely. One team member said, "The anxiety of seeing an email come through from Anne or a phone call . . . your heart would jump."[17] Another admitted to dreading their weekly leadership meetings, bracing for public blowups that could last for hours. Mahlum's success was now creating blind spots.

When you've spent years reinforcing the idea that your intensity is a strength, your vision a gift, your drive a superpower, it becomes nearly impossible to absorb evidence that suggests otherwise. Belief-consistent information processing keeps us seeing what we believe.

What once inspired people was now beginning to burn them out. What once rallied teams was now wearing them down.

When dozens of [solidcore] employees signed a petition calling for Mahlum's resignation, she didn't retreat into defensiveness. Her attention, once fully tuned to growth and momentum, shifted inward. She began to examine the wake she was leaving behind. She invited the board to launch an independent investigation into her leadership. She opened herself to scrutiny. In a company-wide call, she addressed her employees directly. "There's a lot of expectations and responsibilities that come with leadership," Mahlum said on the all-hands. "Not only do I know better than that, but you guys deserve better than that."

The same woman who had built her identity around helping others transform now stood face-to-face with the one transformation she hadn't expected to make: her own. When that moment came, she drew on the same belief that had shaped her father's recovery, her nonprofit, and her company: the belief that transformation is always possible.

Building New Beliefs

Mahlum had done what few visionary founders can: She evolved.

Instead of clinging to the belief that relentless drive was the only path to success, she recognized that sustainable organizations don't just need intensity—they need leaders who can grow with them. She stepped down as CEO of [solidcore] and became executive chairwoman, elevating her COO to the CEO role.

In 2023, Mahlum sold [solidcore], just as she believed she would when she called her shot on that piece of paper ten years earlier. As part of the sale, she awarded millions of dollars to employees, not out of legal obligation, but because she had said she would. "[solidcore]'s success is far from just my own," she said. "It wouldn't be where it is today without a lot of people's commitment."[18]

At every stage, Mahlum's greatest strength was belief: in people, in possibility, in her own ability to shape the world. But even the strongest beliefs, left unchecked, can become blind spots. The very convictions that powered Mahlum's rise eventually needed an upgrade. When we treat beliefs as tools instead of truths, we regain the ability to reshape our attention, respond to reality, and see what others miss.

The First Power of Belief—attention—not only shapes what you see; it shapes what becomes possible. Anne Mahlum proved this three times. First, her beliefs about transformation helped thousands of unhoused people turn their lives around. Then, those same beliefs helped her identify a multimillion-dollar fitness opportunity. She wasn't lucky. She had trained her attention to notice opportunities in plain sight and then worked relentlessly to make change happen. Finally, when it was time for her to change, she recognized that the company needed new leadership and stepped aside instead of insisting she was the only one who could steer it forward.

Mahlum's story teaches us that beliefs that create breakthroughs can also create blind spots. The same conviction that built Back on My Feet and [solidcore] eventually needed updating when her intensity started burning people out instead of energizing them. This is why the most successful people regularly review and refine their beliefs.

You can do the same by asking: What beliefs helped you get where you are today? Which ones still open doors? Which might be quietly closing them? Where are you playing it too safe? Are you doing enough to "provoke luck"?

Your perceptual filters are already at work, quietly determining what you notice and what you miss. The question is whether you're consciously choosing them or letting old programming run on autopilot. Mahlum's greatest insight wasn't about running or fitness. It was recognizing that belief-driven transformation is always possible—including her own. The same is true for your beliefs. They're not fixed. They're tools. And the wisest builders know when it's time to upgrade their toolkits.

Up Next, the Second Power of Belief: Anticipation

If attention shapes what we see in the present, anticipation shapes what we feel about the future. That shift, from perception to prediction, does more than change how we think; it can change how we feel, how we heal, and even how long we live.

In the next chapter, we'll explore how expectations drive emotion, behavior, and biology—and why we so often feel what we believe.

FROM LIMITING BELIEFS...	TO LIBERATING BELIEFS...
Some people are just naturally lucky.	I can create my own luck through how I engage with the world.
Opportunities only come to certain people.	Opportunities are everywhere—I just need to train myself to see them.
People don't really change.	Transformation is possible at any age with the right beliefs and support.
I am who I am.	My identity is a belief I can consciously choose and update.
Questioning myself shows weakness.	Self-reflection is how I stay sharp and continue to grow.

Important Note

You've seen how beliefs shape what you notice and how you interpret the world around you. To help you turn that insight into action, I've prepared exclusive resources—worksheets and attention-training tools that prime your mind to spot opportunities others miss. You'll also gain access to the newest research and strategies that go beyond these pages.

Go to NirAndFar.com/belief-tools/ or scan the QR code below.

THE SECOND POWER OF BELIEF

ANTICIPATION

The Power to **FEEL** What You Believe

Possunt quia posse videntur.
They can because they believe they can.
—VIRGIL, 30 BCE

CHAPTER 5

You Already Live in a Simulation

How to make the ordinary extraordinary (and make a fortune doing it).

L IQUID DEATH. A flaming skull adorns a tallboy aluminum can. Not vodka. Not beer. Not an energy drink. Just water.

In the sanctimonious world of premium hydration, where Evian models frolic in the French Alps, Fiji bottles showcase a tropical paradise, and every brand promises some form of transcendence, Liquid Death arrived like a mohawked punk crashing a meditation retreat. While other brands whisper about "natural minerals" and "artesian wells," Liquid Death screams, "MURDER YOUR THIRST."

The water itself? Surprisingly ordinary. Spring water from the Austrian Alps, yes, but founder Mike Cessario didn't choose the source because of its quality. He chose it because it was the only facility willing to can water instead of bottling it in plastic.[1] The innovation wasn't in the liquid but in the packaging—a deliberate middle finger to an industry that had spent decades making water inoffensive. Liquid Death unified rebellion and virtue signaling by offering consumers a way to express the brand's potent environmental statement: "death to plastic."

Beverage industry experts agreed: It was brand suicide. No parent would buy their child "death" in a can. No retailers would put "death" on the shelf.[2] The entire concept was absurd, juvenile, and doomed to fail.

They couldn't have been more wrong. Liquid Death was no fluke. It was a precisely orchestrated market disruption, built on a sophisticated understanding of how beliefs shape behavior.

When Liquid Death first hit the market in 2019, demand exploded like a Mentos dropped in diet cola. Its first production run of 150,000 cans sold out in under eight weeks.[3] Soon after, Liquid Death was in the top ten bestselling bottled brands on Amazon. By 2021, convenience chains had come aboard, and sales quadrupled to $45 million. Today, Liquid Death is everywhere: Whole Foods, 7-Eleven, Target, Walmart. In 2024, the company was valued at $1.4 billion, and industry watchers speculated about an IPO.

Will Liquid Death stand the test of time? Who knows? A business is more than a product. By the time you read this, it might be another forgotten brand. But whether the company survives is beside the point. What matters is what we can learn from its improbable story. The Liquid Death phenomenon teaches us something important about human behavior—how easily beliefs can transform our experiences.

The Liquid Death saga might look like a triumph of marketing hype, but underneath, it's powered by something more. Cessario understood that if you can shape what someone believes about a product, you can shape how they feel when they experience it, from what they think to what they taste.

"There's not really anything that's incredibly different about our water . . . but there really is nothing incredibly different [about] any product," Cessario told *The Wall Street Journal*.[4] Cessario wasn't selling water; he was engineering a sort of rebellion that, if you knew, you knew. The water just happened to be the medium.

People don't just buy Liquid Death; they proudly post about it on social media. They wear Liquid Death merchandise. Some have even tattooed the brand's logo on their bodies. All this for water that, in blind taste tests, is indistinguishable from countless other brands costing far less.

How can something so objectively ordinary become subjectively extraordinary? The answer lies in the Second Power of Belief: the power of anticipation.

In previous chapters, we explored how beliefs filter our perception of the external world—how they direct our attention and determine what we see. Now we're turning inward to discover how beliefs shape our expectations. They sculpt our emotions, alter how our bodies respond, and even change our moment-to-moment experience of being alive. The central idea is simple but profound: We feel what we believe.

This chapter reveals how companies routinely turn the mundane into the marvelous—and why we'll happily pay extra for the privilege. In later chapters in this section, you'll discover how to harness this same power in your own life: how to reduce suffering, amplify joy, and even trigger physiological changes to extend your lifespan, all by harnessing your beliefs.

To understand this power, we must first explore a radical new understanding of how the brain works. We'll see just how deeply our beliefs color everything we experience.

The Prediction Machine

Throughout history, humans have sought to understand the mind by comparing it to the most advanced technology of their time. In ancient Egypt, doctors sought answers by observing the Nile. They watched the mighty river feed countless channels that transformed barren desert into fertile farmland and believed that the human body worked in a similar way. These early healers viewed the body and mind as a complex network of channels carrying vital fluids, much like their intricate irrigation systems.

Their insight wasn't entirely wrong. These early physicians recognized that vessels extended from the heart to other parts of the body. However, their ideas also led to misguided treatments. When someone showed signs of mental illness, doctors would try to "unclog their channels" with powerful laxatives, a belief and misguided practice that got stuck in the bowels of medical science for thousands of years.[5]

As technology evolved, so did our metaphors for the mind. Plato compared the soul (*psychē*) to a chariot driven by reason and pulled by two horses: one noble and obedient, representing moral impulses, the other fierce and unruly, representing base desires.[6]

René Descartes, surrounded by elaborate mechanical clocks of his time, imagined the brain as a system of pulleys and gears. The Industrial Revolution brought us Sigmund Freud's vision of the mind as a psychological steam engine, with emotions building up pressure in need of release or redirection. We still talk about "letting off steam" to this day, as if our brains are coal-fired boilers.[7]

Postwar innovations brought the DuPont Corporation's promise of "better living through chemistry." Mental health problems were reframed as "chemical imbalances," offering the hope of curing diseases of the mind as easily as adjusting formulas in a test tube. While this led to new treatments of varying efficacy, it oversimplified the complexity of consciousness.[8]

The dawn of computing brought another metaphor. Scientists began to describe the brain as a biological computer, complete with neural circuits and information-processing systems. We now know our brains do not in fact compute information like our laptops. Instead, it turns out that our oldest stories about the nature of consciousness may be the most accurate.

The idea that the world is an illusion appears across cultures and throughout history. Hindu philosophy refers to it as *māyā*—the concept that what we perceive is a cosmic mirage, concealing a deeper reality. Buddhist teachings suggest that our everyday experiences are more akin to dreams created by our minds than accurate representations of what's truly there. Even in Christianity, Judaism, and Islam, many thinkers have viewed the physical world as incomplete—just a stepping stone on the soul's journey to a true and perfect domain.

Modern neuroscience now suggests these philosophical intuitions weren't far off. We each live inside a personalized reality, generated moment by moment in our heads. Your brain is a sophisticated prediction machine, running on what neuroscientists call *predictive processing*.[9] While still a metaphor, the theory explains a crucial aspect of how our minds work.

The key idea is that your subjective experience, whether it's sadness, hunger, or even the taste of canned water, is not directly delivered by your senses. Rather, it's your brain's best prediction about what your sensory input means. As neuroscientist Anil Seth puts it, consciousness is a kind of "controlled hallucination" shaped by belief, memory, and expectation.[10]

Drawing from our lifetime of beliefs, our brains constantly forecast everything we encounter, shaping every moment of our waking lives. Rather than processing eleven million bits of raw sensory data (an impossible task, as we learned in a previous chapter), our brains employ predictive processing to create a simulated world.[11]

We developed this predictive machinery to survive. Thousands of years ago, the speed with which you processed stimuli, like a noise in the bushes, could make the difference between being eaten by a predator and escaping in time. Viscerally recognizing a threat and responding to it instinctively, rather than waiting for our logical minds to catch up, helped our species stay one step ahead.

In our modern world, this ancient system has become a playground for marketers and brands. Companies don't just sell products; they design anticipated experiences, which our predictive machinery helps to fulfill. This cognitive quirk profoundly affects how we enjoy the products we use. It explains why we willingly pay premium prices for ordinary items wrapped in compelling stories.

Wanting What Others Want

What kinds of narratives, then, are most compelling? What makes something desirable?

Sometimes we discover this through direct experience, by trying something and finding that we love it. But more often, we steal our desires from others. We watch what makes people around us light up, what they pursue, what they celebrate. Other people's behavior becomes our shortcut, a signal about what's valuable, and therefore what we should want for ourselves.

This phenomenon is what the French thinker René Girard called "the imitative nature of desire": the idea that we often want something purely because *other people* want it.[12] Your brain instinctively uses social signals as predictive shortcuts. If everyone covets something, your neural circuitry assumes it must have genuine value.

This imitative response likely evolved from our ancestral relationship with scarcity. If your tribe suddenly showed interest in a resource—perhaps a rarely available food or a superior tool material—it signaled something worth pursuing. Our brains learned to act fast: When others desire something, assume it's precious and act quickly to obtain it. In that environment, desires become contagious; the knowledge that others want something spreads far faster than any rational evaluation.

This ancient programming drives our modern consumption patterns, from limited-edition sneaker frenzies to online viral fads. Consider the Stanley Quencher phenomenon of 2023. These $45 insulated water tumblers weren't fundamentally different from countless others. Yet when social media feeds filled with influencers showing off their Stanleys, something remarkable happened. People who had never given a thought to premium drinkware found themselves frantically refreshing websites at midnight for restocks or lining up outside Target stores at the crack of dawn.

What drove the popularity of this particular tumbler? It wasn't due to rational needs—it was thanks to social signals. The perception that "everyone wants this" triggers our imitative desire, a pull that kicks in before conscious thought can intervene. From the Dutch tulip mania in the 1600s to the Tickle Me Elmo riots of 1996 to the GameStop stock frenzy of 2021, we repeatedly fall into the same psychological trap.

To succeed in business, you can either make what people want or make them want what you make. Successful brands start with the former and accelerate with the latter, just as Liquid Death did. They could have manufactured a basic variation on the same bottled water theme. Instead, they manufactured desire through clever anticipation engineering. They designed a new experience for an old product—one that millions would willingly pay for and share with others. The more people shared pictures of Liquid Death on social media or mentioned it to a friend, the more imitative desire kicked in, and the rest is liquid history.

Once we understand how the brain generates experiences based on beliefs, we can start to see this pattern everywhere. Let's examine the mechanics of this powerful process in more detail, breaking it down into four distinct steps.

How to Make People Want What You've Got

Suppose I present you with two glasses of cabernet. I tell you one is a cheap $5 table blend and the other is a $45 premium vintage. The first, less expensive wine is fine, nothing special. It seems a tad flat, perhaps a bit sharp on the finish. The second? Rich and velvety, the wine hints of blackberry and oak. You confidently pronounce that the $45 wine is superior.

But of course, there's a trick: They're the same wine.

In a classic study, researchers used this setup while scanning people's brains in an fMRI machine. When participants believed a wine was expensive, they not only reported enjoying it more; their brains' pleasure centers lit up more strongly, as if the wine literally tasted better.[13]

In this way, your brain is a bit like a Hollywood soundstage: If it expects a high-end experience, it will overlay richer "special effects" to deliver just that. Your brain adds a dash of sophistication, depth, and richness to the flavor because it anticipates that's what a more expensive wine *should* deliver.

Let's use this wine example to guide us along the steps of the Experience Loop, where our minds transform our physical sensations using the Second Power of Belief.

STEP 1: BELIEVE

Our journey begins with belief—not as an opinion but as a frame. Before you feel anything, your brain has already decided what you're likely to feel. It sets the scene in advance. The expectation of tasting an expensive wine creates a mental simulation of exquisite flavor, one your brain treats as real. Anticipated smoothness, richness, complexity… all begin before the first sip. Your brain's prediction machine generates the expected sensations almost instantaneously.

This phenomenon is not limited to wine. Brands often leverage beliefs to frame customer expectations. A "SALE" sign spurs the belief that you're getting an unusual value, triggering excitement before making a purchase. A dizzyingly high luxury price tag signals quality, exclusivity, and prestige, evoking perceptions of superior craftsmanship. A product labeled "NEW!" sparks curiosity, tapping into beliefs about innovation and improvement. The effect is the same: A belief takes hold, and your brain begins simulating how the experience *should* feel.

Liquid Death created an expectation of enjoyment that transformed ordinary water into something more. Rather than just selling hydration, they were selling belief-driven anticipation. Everyone knows water is just water. But when the metal packaging says "Murder Your Thirst" and looks like it belongs on a rock album cover, the belief kicks in: *This is something different.* In the fast-moving world of consumer-packaged goods, different is often believed to be better.

Belief is the first domino in a cascade that ultimately transforms physical sensation.

STEP 2: ANTICIPATE

Once beliefs are leveraged, your brain generates predictions about what comes next. This is where anticipation—nonconscious physiological preparation for the expected experience—takes over.

This step is largely invisible to conscious awareness, even though it leaves clear biological traces. When you believe you're about to taste a premium wine, your brain subtly adjusts on a physical level. In the study of the two identical wines, blood flow in the brain's sensory processing regions changed.

The physiological changes of anticipation prepare your body for what it believes is coming. Don't think of anticipation like a thought along the lines of "this will be good." Rather, it's a reconfiguration of your sensory apparatus to show you that it *is* good.

For Liquid Death, the water becomes secondary to the anticipated experience—a little thrill of rebellion from cracking open a tall, menacing aluminum can emblazoned with a dripping skull and gothic-style font. The company's marketing videos created a mental simulation long before consumers even touched the product. By the time those first units shipped, thousands of people had already played out the whole experience in their heads: imagining bringing Liquid Death to a party, getting reactions ("Wait, you're drinking what?"), feeling ironic or edgy.

In a sense, marketing is about designing simulations: crafting the beliefs and expectations consumers have before they encounter your product or service. The difference between a flop and a phenomenon often lies in the pre-woven story in the customer's mind.

STEP 3: FEEL

Now comes the moment of actual experience—the conscious interpretation of bodily sensations as specific feelings.

When you take the first sip of the "$45" wine, your nervous system is already primed to deliver a premium experience. The subtle notes of oak or berry seem more pronounced. The finish feels longer and more complex. The mouthfeel registers as more balanced and refined. It's the same wine you dismissed five minutes earlier, but now it tastes like something else entirely. Is the wine objectively better? No. It's chemically identical to the "cheap" version. But your experience is genuinely different, because your brain expected it to be.

This isn't pretending or performing. You're not acting when you express greater enjoyment of the expensive wine. You're describing your actual experience, which your beliefs and anticipation have fundamentally altered.

This phenomenon extends to countless domains. Participants in a coffee study were told they were drinking either caffeinated or decaffeinated coffee. In reality, both groups received only decaf. Yet those who believed they were consuming caffeine reported feeling more alert and even performed better on attention tasks.[14] Belief alone can lead to an anticipatory response (increased heart rate, higher blood pressure) that resembles the effects of actual caffeine.

When golfers believed they were using a professional player's putter versus an ordinary one, they performed significantly better, requiring fewer strokes on the green.[15] The belief in the "superior" equipment led to anticipatory changes in muscle tension and focus, resulting in actual performance improvements.

Even in medicine, the effect is striking. In one study on headaches, patients reported significantly more relief when taking branded pills versus generic ones, even though the pills were chemically identical.[16] The premium brand created anticipation of superior relief, altering how the body processes and responds to the medication, creating a genuinely different feeling, which patients confirm by reporting better outcomes.

STEP 4: CONFIRM

Once you've had the experience, your brain looks for resolution. Was it what you expected? Did the story hold up? The final step closes and reinforces the loop through conscious reflection and social affirmation.

After tasting the "superior," expensive wine, you may think to yourself, "You really can taste the complexity," or "This is so much smoother than the cheap stuff." More than just describing your experience, these thoughts reinforce and strengthen your original belief.

When you share your experience with others, you're solidifying neural pathways that strengthen the price-quality connection in your brain. Wine enthusiasts gather to confirm each other's opinions and nod along with reviewers' tasting notes. The confirmation step helps beliefs crystallize, transforming a sip into a lasting mental model that shapes future experiences. We don't just feel differently—we think differently.

THE EXPERIENCE LOOP

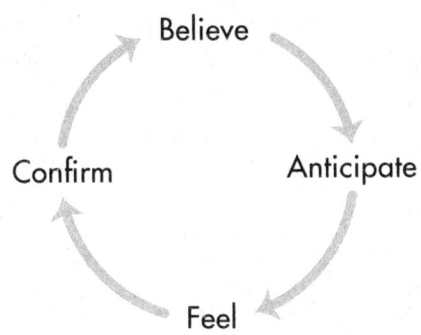

A self-reinforcing cycle that changes the way we experience the products we use.

Sometimes marketers take an even more direct approach to shaping the Experience Loop. Consider the famous Lay's potato chips slogan: "Bet you can't eat just one." More than a memorable line, it's a deliberate suggestion that plants a specific belief about your future behavior. By telling us we won't be able to stop, the phrase makes us anticipate the feeling of wanting more, so we do.

This aligns with psychiatrist Scott Alexander's suggestion that addiction might be understood as "what happens when you become hyper-aware of one particular facet of your normal motivation system."[17] We anticipate irresistibility, our attention zeroes in on the craving sensation, and consequently we experience the chips as more compelling than they really are.

These psychological triggers aren't limited to explicit suggestions of irresistibility. Beliefs can make or break a brand's success, sometimes far more surely than objective factors. In the mid-1990s, Toyota and General Motors sold virtually the same car under two different brands. Off the assembly line rolled twins: the Toyota Corolla and the Geo Prizm. They had the same engine, same chassis, much of the same design—essentially clones with different badges.

Yet when J.D. Power surveyed owners, the Toyota Corolla consistently ranked higher in quality and owner satisfaction than the Geo Prizm. In one study of initial quality, the Corolla was rated as the tenth best-built car in America, while its twin, the Prizm, lagged at twenty-eighth.[18]

Toyota had spent decades cultivating a reputation for bulletproof reliability. Geo, a relatively new GM sub-brand, had no such history. Corolla owners, who believed in Toyota's quality and anticipated a superior experience, genuinely felt that the car was better built. Prizm owners, without those beliefs, interpreted identical mechanical noises as worrisome, the same manual shifter as clunky, and the same interior materials as cheaper. Their feelings about identical cars were dramatically different.

That is what happens when we interpret our physiological reactions through the lens of our beliefs. Our beliefs inform what we anticipate, which shapes how we feel; we then consciously confirm these feelings, and the cycle continues.

In marketing, an ad campaign is considered successful if it persuades someone to purchase the product. But the truly masterful campaigns create an expectation that enhances the experience of the product itself, setting the stage for the performance.

But isn't this all just fancy deception? Not necessarily. When a brand makes a mundane experience fun or meaningful, that's genuine value. Drinking water from a can branded with a message that resonates with you is more enjoyable than sipping from a flimsy bottle—the joy is real, even if it's "all in your head." As long as the company delivers on its basic promises (Liquid Death's water is pure, refreshing, and not sold in plastic bottles), the extra enjoyment layered on through clever anticipation-building is a bonus, not a scam.

We often know at some level that we're being romanced by marketing, but we participate willingly because it makes life a bit more enjoyable. We all know Liquid Death isn't objectively better than generic water, but its edgy, irreverent humor and eco-messaging transform ordinary hydration into a statement.

Successful brands are expectation engines. When they run well, everyone involved feels the difference.

Selective Skepticism

If our brain constantly shapes not only what we see but also what we feel based on our beliefs, wouldn't the rational response be to question everything? How much should we doubt our expectations? Should we second-guess every craving, every assumption, every gut feeling?

Not exactly. There's a more nuanced approach that serves us better—what I call selective skepticism. This is the art of knowing when to question your beliefs and when to accept them, even if they may not be entirely accurate.

Selective skepticism doesn't mean cynicism. We shouldn't try to debunk every source of joy in our lives. That would be miserable, like peeling all the paint off a beautiful painting to see the canvas underneath. Some beliefs and harmless illusions genuinely enrich our lives, with no serious downsides.

If you enjoy your premium headphones, that experience has real value, which doesn't need to be dissected. Who among us actually knows if $500 headphones sound better than a $100 pair? Whatever the ad copy claims about superior components, a better fit, or cutting-edge acoustic science, research consistently shows that consumers can't reliably distinguish between high-end and mid-range headphones in blind tests.[19] But assuming you can afford the fancier set, go for it! Real life isn't a blind test. You'd likely enjoy the name brand more.

Here's a useful self-check in these situations. Ask yourself: Is this belief serving me, or am I serving it?

If a belief is serving you—by adding delight, motivation, focus, or connection—there's no need to shatter it. You might be fully aware that much of the joy is in the belief, and that's fine.

On the flip side, some beliefs actively drain us. If you're exhausting yourself maintaining a perfect social media image or avoiding new opportunities because you "can't handle change," it's time to question those assumptions. Your negative anticipation is sabotaging your actual experience.

In other words, we need selective skepticism: the wisdom to know when an anticipated experience is leading us astray, and when it is harmless or even beneficial.

Sometimes our preconceptions cheat us out of fresh experiences. If you assume a meeting will be useless, you might mentally check out and indeed get nothing from it. The anticipation of uselessness becomes self-fulfilling. If you believe a person you just met isn't likable, you might give off cold vibes that make them less inclined to show their good side, confirming your negative belief.

In these cases, a little skepticism toward your own beliefs can save you. Maybe there's a key insight in that dull meeting, if you listen closely. Perhaps the person you initially pegged as unfriendly turned out to be shy, and a warmer approach would have drawn out a great conversation.

Identify areas where your anticipatory beliefs might be limiting you. Negative emotions like dread, resentment, and prejudice can be red flags that a belief deserves examining. Try using selective skepticism in small moments:

- If you dread Mondays at work, question what you're anticipating. Ask yourself: Is it as bad as I projected on Sunday night, or am I amplifying a narrative? By examining the story, you may find ways to reshape your expectations and transform your experience. Perhaps instead of saying "Mondays are miserable," you can reframe it as "Mondays are a fresh start."
- Before you hit "buy" on that expensive gadget that seems life-changing, ask: Am I in love with the thing itself, or just the story around it? Sometimes even pausing can break the spell. Financial expert Paco de Leon, author of *Finance for the People*, suggests using a "buy list." Write it down, wait two weeks, then see if you still want to purchase it.[20]
- Question negative assumptions like "It can't be done." Rather than accepting those beliefs, look for the fastest, cheapest way to learn whether your beliefs and assumptions are true. Before Liquid Death became a product, Cessario tested whether the company's "Murder Your Thirst" approach would resonate using

a low-budget mockup on Facebook and an online commercial. Turns out, it did.

You Are a Simulation Designer

If our beliefs determine what we feel, then we can consciously design our own experiences from the inside out. Every day, whether you realize it or not, you're constructing simulations. You build them for yourself. You build them for others. With every expectation you set, every story you tell, you're shaping how the moment will feel before it arrives.

If you lead a team, you are designing the "simulation" your employees step into each morning. The culture you create shapes what people anticipate will happen in the workplace. Their expectations, in turn, become their daily work experience. If you work in marketing, product design, or customer experience, you're already in the simulation business. Every touchpoint is an opportunity to build a new simulation in your customers' minds.

One of the most powerful tools in this process is the use of evocative language to transform ordinary offerings into anticipated experiences. Netflix doesn't offer "video access subscriptions." It invites you to "See What's Next," setting the expectation of boundless discovery and enjoyment. Adidas doesn't sell "athletic gear." They channel Muhammad Ali's defiant declaration "Impossible Is Nothing," transforming sportswear into manifestos of personal power. Airbnb doesn't list "temporary accommodations." They help you "Belong Anywhere," reframing a simple night's stay into an experience of connection.

In my experience with my last book, *Indistractable*, I noticed a clear difference between leaders who shared my techniques with colleagues as part of a "productivity initiative" and those who shared them as a way to become "masters of your time and attention." The first demands compliance. The second creates anticipation of personal empowerment. Leaders who chose the latter approach had more excited employees and better results. The choice of language changes people's experience even before they've shown up—reprogramming the simulation itself.

You are also the designer of your personal simulations. If you've always believed you hate networking events, you'll likely go into them anticipating awkwardness and leave feeling your time was wasted. But what if you consciously set a different expectation? Before the next event, you might tell yourself, "I'll uncover at least one interesting story tonight." That minor tweak can change what you notice and how you feel during the event. You've rewritten the simulation script for a better experience ahead.

The most important simulation you'll ever design is your daily experience. Most of us let our anticipations run on autopilot, shaped by habit, environment, and unexamined beliefs. Understanding that our beliefs shape our experience gives us the power to transform mundane moments into meaningful ones, find joy in boredom, and discover opportunities in obstacles.

But what if it could go further? Could the same mechanisms change how we feel physical pain? Could they stretch the boundaries of what our bodies are capable of? Could they even extend our lives?

FROM LIMITING BELIEFS...	TO LIBERATING BELIEFS...
My feelings are real, valid, and objective.	What I feel comes from what I believe, not just from the situation itself.
My feelings are automatic reactions I can't control.	I can influence my feelings by setting different expectations.
I need to change my circumstances, situation, or environment to feel better.	I can transform ordinary moments by changing the story I bring to them.
Marketing is just manipulation and lies.	Smart marketing creates anticipation that enhances the product experience.
Expensive means better.	Beliefs often shape my experience more than the product itself.

CHAPTER 6

Sickness Is in the Body; Illness Is in the Mind

Not all pain is necessary.

SIMON CALLED IT the "carousel of pain." It seemed to move unpredictably throughout his body. "One day my shoulder would hurt . . . and I'd pray, 'If only this pain could go away.' Then it would go away—but move to my foot."[1]

After multiple examinations and tests ruled out structural causes, doctors diagnosed him with fibromyalgia. "It's an exclusion diagnosis," he notes. "There's no machine that beeps and says, 'You have fibromyalgia.' They've just excluded everything else." While the diagnosis initially provided some assurance, it came with a devastating caveat: "It's incurable."

Simon's descent into chronic pain wasn't sudden. Years of conventional treatments provided minimal relief. Medications reduced his pain from sevens, eights, and nines down to fours, fives, and sixes, but this plateau became his new normal—a lifetime sentence of constant discomfort. He avoided anything that might worsen his pain: socializing with friends, dating, or any activity beyond his front door. "So

I isolated more and more," he recalls. "I was basically a hermit at that point—avoidance, avoidance, avoidance."

But the pain didn't stop.

Desperate for answers, Simon spent over $20,000 on specialized physical therapy. When that approach ultimately failed, he felt abandoned and rejected. "I couldn't move, I couldn't do anything. Watching TV, immobile in my bed, was excruciating."

The turning point came at a Christmas party (which he remembers struggling even to attend), where he met a woman who offhandedly mentioned that she recovered from fibromyalgia years earlier by solely changing her mind rather than her body. For the first time, Simon began to consider that his pain might not be permanent. He was introduced to a new way of dealing with his pain, which swapped his old beliefs about the nature of pain with a new understanding. Within just four months of adopting these new beliefs, Simon described himself as "over chronic pain"—the carousel had finally stopped.

Simon's recovery poses profound questions. What if our conventional wisdom about how we handle pain is flawed? The standard protocol tells us to avoid triggers, rest, and cease activity, just as Simon did. We're taught to treat pain as an enemy to be feared and sedated away as soon as possible. But what if this defensive stance actually amplifies our suffering? What if our beliefs about pain are making us hurt more than is necessary?

Most importantly, if belief can reshape our experience of pain, what other aspects of our physical and mental well-being might be similarly malleable? To understand what might be possible, we need to examine the neural mechanisms at work.

The Brain on Pain

A volunteer lay inside an fMRI machine as researchers applied searing heat to his forearm while scanning his brain. The researchers had instructed him to remain perfectly still despite the pain, as any movement would blur the brain images they were capturing. "Eight out of ten," he winced, rating his discomfort.[2]

After several excruciating rounds, a lab technician approached with a small white jar with pharmaceutical markings. "This is a powerful analgesic cream," he explained. "It contains a local pain reducer that will substantially decrease the sensation."

The volunteer watched hopefully as the technician applied the cream to his reddened skin. He'd used prescription analgesics before, and he knew they worked. As the machine hummed back to life and he slid into the narrow tube again, he felt a wave of relief.

When the next heat pulse began, something remarkable happened. "Maybe a four out of ten," he reported when asked to rate the pain. "I can still feel the heat, but it doesn't really hurt like before."

What he didn't know—what none of the participants in Dr. Tor Wager's groundbreaking study knew—was that the "powerful analgesic" was ordinary hand lotion from the university bookstore. The jar contained no active ingredients whatsoever. Yet his pain was cut in half.

Inside the control room, researchers watched something extraordinary unfold on their monitors. The brain scans revealed two different neurological responses to the same level of heat. Without the lotion, the brain's pain-processing centers lit up with activity when heat was applied. With the lotion, despite precisely the same level of heat, those same brain regions showed decreased activity. The application of that completely nonmedical skin cream had another measurable effect: The volunteer's prefrontal cortex, the brain region involved in expectations and predictions, became more active, dampening his pain response.

Across dozens of participants in Wager's study, the same pattern emerged. Believing in the effects of analgesic cream significantly reduced both reported pain and brain activity in pain-processing regions. The effect wasn't due to any change at the skin level: The brain itself interpreted the pain differently.

Published in the leading journal *Science*, Wager's landmark study on the placebo effect provided evidence that expectations can alter how the brain processes pain.[3] As Wager would later explain, "The brain has its own internal pharmacy." In other words, the mere *belief* that you're receiving an effective treatment can cause your brain to release natural painkillers.[4]

Wager's studies demonstrate an idea we saw in the last chapter: the capacity of anticipation, the Second Power of Belief, to transform physical experience. Our brain interprets incoming signals based on what it expects to feel. When we anticipate relief, our brains make it so. When we anticipate discomfort, we suffer more.

In the previous chapter, we examined how beliefs influence taste and enjoyment through the Experience Loop. The same mechanism that makes expensive wine and branded water taste better also holds in the context of pain:

1. **Believe:** In Wager's placebo study, the volunteers had reason to believe the cream would reduce pain.

2. **Anticipate:** This belief triggered anticipation, as their brains physiologically prepared for reduced pain, adjusting their sensitivity before the heat stimulus even arrived.

3. **Feel:** Wager's participants reported less discomfort and showed lower pain-processing activity in their brains. The change in expectations changed how their brains processed the sensation.

4. **Confirm:** The participants' verbal reports of reduced pain confirmed the effectiveness of the "analgesic" cream, reinforcing a belief that would shape future experiences.

This pattern shows up in both clinical and everyday contexts. From chronic pain to everyday discomforts, our beliefs shape how we approach challenges. It can even give us the edge to face the difficult tasks we know matter most, but rarely feel motivated to do.

Motivation Is Pain Management

We tell ourselves small, comforting lies all the time:

"I'll start working out tomorrow when I have more energy."

"I'll have that difficult conversation next week when the timing is better."

"I'll get that big project off the ground once I feel more motivated."

We've all made such promises, only to repeat them day after day without following through. The structure is the same: Once I get motivated, I'll take action.

But what if our approach to motivation is fundamentally backward?

We think we're waiting for motivation. But motivation doesn't show up first—discomfort does.

Think about why we eat. We don't consume food simply because it's pleasant (though it can be), but because the gnawing craving in our stomach is uncomfortable. Even when we're not physically hungry, the craving for delicious food is psychologically distressing. (No need to tell that to a former fat kid.) Wanting hurts. As Sean Mackey, chief of the Stanford Division of Pain Medicine, puts it, "Pain is the great motivator."[5] Motivation itself is a system for managing discomfort.

When we procrastinate—putting off exercise, difficult conversations, or challenging work—we're not failing at finding motivation; we're avoiding anticipated discomfort. Our brain predicts that the workout will hurt, the conversation will feel awkward, or the mental effort will strain us. This anticipation creates an immediate urge to disengage from the activity.

Unfortunately, our predictions are often wrong. We tend to overestimate how long unpleasant sensations will last.[6] The more intense the anticipated discomfort, the less likely we are to engage, even when the actual experience proves far less unpleasant than expected.

"Anticipatory anxiety is almost always worse than the thing itself," according to researcher Ethan Kross.[7] We might think that anxiety prepares us to confront disaster, but in fact, "worst-case mental models . . . themselves become barriers to action." Exaggerated predictions can keep us stuck.

Think of what this means for your own life. Each time you avoid exercise because you anticipate it will hurt, you're strengthening neural associations between exercise and negative feelings. The avoidance itself reinforces the anticipated discomfort, creating a self-perpetuating cycle that makes future attempts even more difficult.

But Wager's hand lotion placebo study reveals the flip side of this cycle: Just as negative anticipations make experiences feel worse, positive anticipations can make them feel better—or at least less painful. In one study, runners who were taught to adopt a neutral, observational mindset toward the burning sensation in their lungs and legs performed significantly better.[8] In another study, when runners were cued to relax and maintain a light smile during effortful running, they showed better performance and reported lower discomfort, even at the same exertion levels.[9] These runners weren't denying their sensations; they were simply reframing them.

Applying this insight to your own challenges means recognizing that discomfort isn't something to be avoided, but just another belief to reconsider. The key to motivation is changing how you anticipate and interpret the inevitable discomfort that comes with growth.

When I was working on my last book, I noticed how my mind would find excuses for procrastinating: "I need more research first"; "I should refine the outline a bit more"; "I'll just answer these emails before starting." This led me to reorganize my research notes, open browser tabs, and dive into low-stakes tasks, taking me away from my goal of completing a chapter. Eventually, I realized I was dodging the discomfort of concentrated effort that came with wrestling complex ideas into clear, coherent paragraphs.

Once I recognized this pattern, I stopped trying to eliminate this discomfort. Instead, I changed my relationship with it, viewing those feelings of resistance as signals that I was about to do important, meaningful work. This mental shift didn't make writing effortless, but it made the struggle feel purposeful. It transformed my experience of the challenge, making it less painful, and I became more productive as a result. I only learned to manage procrastination when I learned to manage my pain.

Predicting Pain

For Simon, overcoming his chronic pain gave him his life back. But to do it, he had to unlearn everything he believed about his symptoms, starting with the source of his pain.

Most of us assume that pain is caused by damage in the body, but that's often not the case. When you touch a hot stove, specialized nerve endings in your finger, called nociceptors, send signals to your brain. But those signals aren't pain. They're just raw data. Your brain interprets them, weaving in context, memory, and belief to conduct an instant threat assessment and create the conscious experience of hurt. The detection occurs in the periphery, but the subjective sensation of pain is always generated in the brain.

This is why researchers increasingly speak of "neuroplastic pain": pain sustained not by injury, but by the brain's own predictions. As pain psychologist Alan Gordon explains, "The brain learns to predict pain to protect you. But sometimes these predictions become overprotective, warning you of danger even when there's no tissue damage occurring."[10]

Neuroplastic pain is the brain's overfixation on what it believes is potential future damage. Those false alarms trap people in a pain-fear-pain cycle. Gordon explains it with stark clarity: "When we respond to pain with fear, it reinforces that it's dangerous, and the pain persists. Fear is the fuel for the pain."

The result is a cruel loop. The anticipation of discomfort creates suffering by amplifying symptoms; avoidance only strengthens the cycle. Every time we retreat from pain, we reinforce the brain's mistaken belief.

Gordon's own back pain illustrates this cycle. After a minor injury and sufficient healing time, his MRI results came back normal. Yet his pain remained, sharp and debilitating, whenever he sat down. The problem wasn't his back. It was his brain.

Merely anticipating a long meeting would trigger anxiety, which in turn amplified pain when he sat down. His brain had learned to associate sitting with danger: another example of a pain-fear-pain cycle driven not by tissue damage but by expectation.

Neuroimaging studies support this model. In patients with chronic pain, researchers have found heightened activity in brain regions associated with emotional processing and prediction during pain experiences, while areas that process raw sensory signals are less active.[11] In effect, the brain shifts from primarily responding to tissue damage to mainly responding to the pain it expects—and to the fear it generates.

Pain Turnarounds

Understanding that much of chronic pain is driven by prediction rather than actual tissue damage opens up a powerful possibility. If the brain can learn to expect pain, it can also learn to expect safety. Pain turnarounds are moments when a person breaks the pain-fear-pain cycle and replaces it with a new pattern that leads to relief.

After Simon attended the Christmas party, he started practicing pain reprocessing therapy (PRT) to reprogram his fearful beliefs. Like the turnaround method we explored in chapter 3, PRT asks us to question our automatic interpretations and systematically retrain our brains' predictive patterns through three key components:

1. **Observation:** Notice sensations with curiosity rather than fear. Instead of labeling them as pain, describe them in neutral terms: pressure, warmth, tingling. This disrupts the automatic threat detection and fear response that amplifies the perception of pain.

2. **Safety reappraisal:** Look for evidence that the sensation is *not* a sign of damage. If movement were truly harmful, pain wouldn't disappear when your stress level drops or your attention shifts.

3. **Positive affect:** Use humor or lightness to challenge old predictions. One of Gordon's patients responded to pain during safe movement with, "Nice try, brain—I know this isn't dangerous."

In a randomized controlled trial published in *JAMA Psychiatry*, 66 percent of patients with chronic back pain were pain-free or nearly pain-free after four weeks of PRT, compared to 20 percent in the placebo group and 10 percent receiving usual care.[12]

These same techniques can also help in situations where anticipated discomfort prevents beneficial action. If you avoid public speaking because you fear humiliation, procrastinate on difficult work because you anticipate mental strain, or skip exercise because you expect physical discomfort, you're caught in your own prediction loop. By observing sensations without catastrophic labels, reappraising their meaning, and pairing them with positive emotion, you can change what you anticipate—and with it, what you feel.

You don't need a formal therapy program to create this kind of shift. Sometimes simply believing that relief is possible, with or without active medication, is enough.

Illness Is Not Sickness

The body's natural healing processes, rather than drugs or procedures, do most of the work in maintaining our health. According to Dr. Wayne Jonas, approximately 80 percent of what keeps populations healthy stems from our own restorative abilities, which are activated by our daily behaviors, relationships, and the degree to which we find our treatments meaningful. Medical interventions, such as pharmaceuticals and surgeries, contribute only 15 to 20 percent to overall health, yet they account for 80 to 90 percent of healthcare spending.[13]

Modern medicine excels at treating immediate dangers like infections and injuries. However, it often falls short with chronic conditions like depression, migraines, and persistent pain, the very conditions that cost us the most.

This gap highlights a problem with our approach to recovery. When we dismiss the body's self-healing abilities as "just a placebo" and treat them as somehow less legitimate than pharmaceutical or surgical interventions, we ignore one of our most effective ways to reduce suffering.

How do we make sense of the placebo effect? What can it do and what are its limits? Placebos aren't miracle cures that can overcome any disease on their own. The science shows a more nuanced reality: Placebos work powerfully on subjective experiences like pain, anxiety, fatigue, and mood, but have little to no effect on underlying structural diseases or objective physiological functions.

To distinguish between the two, it is helpful to consider the distinction between illness and sickness. As James Alcock explains, "Feeling ill is not the same as being sick. Whereas disease (sickness) refers to biological dysfunction, illness refers to the experience of bodily symptoms, which may or may not reflect disease. Illness is influenced by our beliefs about disease, our cultural interpretation of symptoms, our biases and emotional needs, and even by self-delusion."[14]

Just as someone can have a disease without feeling ill (like having early-stage cancer without symptoms), we can also experience illness (such as pain) without having any underlying disease. Our subjective experience of symptoms doesn't always match our objective biological state.

This distinction helps explain why placebos can dramatically improve how sick people feel, even without altering the underlying disease. Your subjective experience of symptoms can change dramatically even when the pathophysiology remains the same.

Consider a revealing study published in *The New England Journal of Medicine*. Researchers assigned asthma patients to one of four interventions: an albuterol inhaler (an effective medication), a placebo inhaler, placebo acupuncture, or no treatment.

When patients rated their own improvement, the real medication and the placebo interventions produced nearly identical subjective benefits: Patients felt significantly better with all three treatments compared to no treatment. But when the researchers objectively measured the patients' lung function, they found something very different: Only the albuterol inhaler produced actual improvement in breathing capacity.[15]

When you receive a treatment you believe will help, even if it's a placebo, your brain releases endorphins—natural painkillers—and dopamine, which is associated with reward and relief. These neurochemical changes significantly alter the way you perceive and respond to pain and discomfort.

Even more remarkably, placebo responses can be specific to different types of pain. When participants received identical placebos but were told some were like morphine (good for sharp pain) and others like aspirin (good for inflammatory pain), their relief mirrored that of the drug they believed they'd taken.[16]

Perhaps the most dramatic demonstrations of the power of placebos come from surgery studies. Researchers compared real arthroscopic knee surgeries for osteoarthritis against sham procedures where surgeons made incisions but performed no actual repair. Patients who received the sham surgery reported pain relief and functional improvement identical to those who had the real procedure—and these benefits lasted for years.[17]

Think of the truth demonstrated by these placebo studies. For conditions where pain is the primary symptom, changing our expectations can dramatically alter what we feel, even when the underlying structural condition remains unchanged.

Understanding these boundaries is crucial. While placebos can significantly reduce suffering, promoting them as replacements for evidence-based treatments for disease—rather than illness—crosses a line. But for those conditions in which subjective experience is the central problem, placebo responses can be remarkably beneficial. The optimal approach isn't choosing between placebos and "real" medicine, but intelligently combining them to maximize benefit while minimizing suffering.

Honest Placebos

For most of medical history, using placebos depended on some level of deception. Doctors prescribed an inert treatment without telling the patient it contained no active ingredient. This created an ethical dilemma: Harnessing placebo effects meant misleading patients and violating informed-consent principles.

But what if deception isn't actually necessary? What if placebos can work even when patients know exactly what they're taking?

Ted Kaptchuk, director of Harvard Medical School's Program in Placebo Studies, decided to test this unorthodox idea. He recruited eighty patients with irritable bowel syndrome (IBS) and gave half no treatment and half placebos. But instead of deceiving the members of this second group, Kaptchuk gave them pills clearly labeled PLACEBO. He explicitly told them that the placebo pills were "made of an inert substance, like sugar pills, that had been shown in clinical studies to produce significant improvement in IBS symptoms through mind-body self-healing processes."[18]

Before patients were asked to consent, researchers carefully explained how placebos could work through conditioning, expectancy, and biological responses to pill-taking rituals. Patients were instructed to take these "open-label" placebos twice daily.

The results were remarkable. After three weeks, the open-label placebo group reported significantly greater improvement in IBS symptoms than the no-treatment group. The magnitude of improvement was comparable to effects from powerful IBS medications assessed in other clinical trials.

"We were stunned," Kaptchuk admitted. "We had hoped it would work, but the size of the effect was larger than we expected."[19]

A range of studies suggest that placebos for pain relief are growing more effective over time, possibly due to increasing public awareness of the placebo effect itself.[20] The placebo effect appears to be fueled by its own publicity: The more we hear about placebos working, the better they work. But this creates a paradox. If the first step in the Experience Loop's Believe-Anticipate-Feel-Confirm cycle is belief, how can placebos work when patients know they're receiving inert substances?

The answer lies in the way our brains process information on multiple levels. Even when our rational mind knows a treatment is "just a placebo," other brain systems, particularly those involved in unconscious learning and conditioning, continue to respond to the ritual and context of treatment.

Consider your emotional response to watching a great movie. You know the film is fictional, but your blood pressure might still rise during suspenseful moments and your eyes might well up during a sad scene. Our brains evolved to respond to patterns and associations before engaging in rational analysis, allowing both processes to coexist without resolving their contradictions.

Placebos take advantage of this fact. The ritual of taking a pill—from noticing the shape of the pill to grabbing it from the bottle and swallowing it—calls up a set of unconscious patterns and associations. These cues trigger responses in your body, even when you know you're taking an inert treatment. Your thinking mind knows there's no active ingredient in the pill, but your body's automatic systems still respond favorably to the familiar act of taking medicine. The relief that follows then closes the Experience Loop, confirming your expectation and reinforcing your belief in the placebo for next time.

This removes the false dichotomy between "real medicine" and "just the placebo effect." It suggests we can ethically harness placebo effects to manage pain and discomfort in daily life with or without self-deception.

Seen this way, many of the remedies people swear by—vitamin C tablets, herbal supplements, and daily tonics—might be working primarily through belief and anticipation rather than direct biochemical action. A search on Amazon turns up several brands of "placebo pills," some boasting hundreds of five-star reviews and testimonials praising fast-acting relief. If a safe and affordable intervention improves your life, maybe that's all that matters.

Throw Some Ass

In 2018, Sophie Hawley-Weld, member of the Grammy-nominated electronic music duo Sofi Tukker, was in the midst of a whirlwind year: releasing her first album, launching a new record label, and touring nonstop with countless late nights. The pace was exhilarating—and exhausting. During her year of touring, Hawley-Weld began to experience debilitating chronic migraines and persistent back pain that forced her to retreat to dark rooms.

She tried every treatment she could find, but nothing worked. Doctors recommended cortisone injections for her back, which only intensified her fear and worsened her condition—a phenomenon well documented in pain studies.

Like many people with chronic pain, Hawley-Weld began avoiding anything that might make it worse. Her brain learned to believe that movement was dangerous, locking her into a cycle of fear, bracing, and confirmation: Each painful or tense moment reinforced the belief that her body was fragile.[21]

Her turning point came in the most unlikely place: a choreography rehearsal. Her Brazilian dancer friends convinced her to try a move she found awkward and uncomfortable: "throwing her ass." Hawley-Weld hesitated. "I'm so uncomfortable with this. I don't know how to do it. I don't want to do it," she told her dancers. But they wouldn't let it go, encouraging her to try. She braced for the pain she was certain would follow.

Yet there was none: a jarring break between what her brain expected and what her body delivered. Instead of pain, she felt playful and, most importantly, safe. It was one of the first moments that made her question the belief that movement was dangerous.

She repeated the movement again, and again, each time without pain. Slowly, the old loop (movement is dangerous → anticipate pain → feel pain → confirm danger) was replaced with a new one (movement can be safe → anticipate relief → feel ease → confirm capability).

That breakthrough inspired a celebratory dance track called "Throw Some Ass," which Hawley-Weld explains is about the "mind-body connection."

The refrain, "Throw some ass, free the mind," captured what she had discovered: Sometimes the fastest way to quiet the brain's alarm system is to do something joyful with your body. The rhythm, the coordination, and the sheer fun of the moment consumed her attention. That absence of hypervigilance gave her nervous system a powerful new message: *This is safe.* As she puts it, "When you do something ridiculous with your body and feel free and happy, it can make the pain go away."

Just as the placebo studies showed, change begins in anticipation—in what the brain expects will happen next. Each time Hawley-Weld repeated the move without pain, she chipped away at the belief that movement was dangerous and built evidence that it was harmless. By pairing movement with safety and joy, she was doing exactly what a powerful placebo does: changing what the brain anticipates, and with it, what the body feels. No pill required.

Turning Belief into Relief

Hawley-Weld didn't need a prescription to change what her body felt. She simply needed an experience strong enough to replace an old belief with a new one, and to confirm it again and again until it stuck.

You can design your own "placebos": experiences, rituals, or other cues that update what your brain anticipates and, consequently, what you feel. Here's what the research shows about how to make them work for you.

1. **Delivery:** The form of a placebo matters.
    - Pills are most effective for managing pain and sleep issues, while creams and balms are better suited for localized discomfort.
    - Larger pills produce stronger effects than smaller ones, and capsules tend to outperform tablets.

2. **Dose:** More placebo can sometimes yield better results.
    - Research shows two placebo pills work better than one, and taking them more than once a day can amplify effects.[22]
    - The act of taking a treatment at consistent times builds a predictive loop; your brain starts preparing for the relief before it arrives.

3. **Association (conditioning):** Pair relief with a cue your brain can learn.
   - In one study, pairing pain medication with a distinctive-tasting drink trained participants' brains to expect relief. Later, the drink alone, without medication, still significantly reduced pain.[23]
   - This is classical conditioning: Your brain links the cue to relief and runs the program automatically.

4. **Design:** Make it look, taste, and sound like it works.
   - Red and orange pills seem to work better as stimulants, while blue and green pills seem to make better sedatives.[24]
   - White pills are perceived as safer but less potent.[25]
   - Bitter-tasting liquids are perceived as more medicinal and often produce more potent effects than sweet ones.[26]

5. **Scripts:** What you say shapes what you feel.
   - The language surrounding a placebo dramatically influences its effectiveness. For example, "This placebo pill will help my body activate its natural pain-relieving mechanisms."
   - Describing a placebo as a powerful pain reliever that works for most people produces significantly stronger effects than neutral descriptions.[27]

6. **Social reinforcement:** Relief loves company.
   - Placebo effects are amplified when someone else administers the treatment rather than when you do it yourself.[28]
   - Knowing that others have benefited from the same treatment enhances the placebo effect.

Using placebos this way means intentionally leveraging your brain's natural ability to modulate pain and discomfort through the power of anticipation. The beauty of honest placebos is that they can work even when you know they're placebos.

With this understanding, you'll start noticing the placebo effect everywhere. A favorite mug that makes coffee somehow taste better. A friend's reassuring hand on your shoulder that relieves your anxiety. A breath that steadies you before you speak. Each one is a reminder that your experience is never fixed. It's shaped, moment to moment, by what you expect to feel.

Feel Good Now

The most powerful changes in your body often start with the narrative in your mind: how you interpret the present and anticipate the future.

Imagine believing that the burning sensation in your lungs during your run isn't a signal to stop, but evidence you're growing stronger. Picture reframing the tension before a difficult conversation not as anxiety to be avoided, but as energy being mobilized to help you connect. Consider treating the mental strain of focus not as suffering, but as the sensation of your brain building new capabilities.

Every time you reframe discomfort, create a meaningful ritual, or simply observe sensations with curiosity instead of fear, you're changing your perspective. You're reshaping the neural circuits that define your physical experience.

Your body isn't just something you have; it's something you create, every moment, through the power of anticipation. But the power of anticipatory beliefs extends beyond managing pain or reframing discomfort. What happens when these same mechanisms influence how you age, how you heal, and perhaps even how long you live?

In the next chapter, we'll explore the surprising connections between your expectations and your most fundamental biological processes. We'll separate extraordinary scientific discoveries from wishful thinking and reveal how simple shifts in how you think about your body can unlock capabilities you never knew you had.

FROM LIMITING BELIEFS...	TO LIBERATING BELIEFS...
All pain means physiological damage.	Pain is a signal shaped by the brain, not always proof of injury.
Placebo effects are fake.	Placebos can work even when you know they're placebos.
How you feel always reflects what's biologically wrong.	Illness (how you feel) is different from sickness (biological disease)—and they don't always line up.
Discomfort should always be avoided.	Discomfort is information I can observe with curiosity.
I'm stuck with my pain.	Through new beliefs, I can retrain my brain and reshape how I experience pain.

CHAPTER 7

Living Longer, Stronger, and Smarter

Your beliefs can become your biology.

T HE SIXTY-SEVEN-YEAR-OLD'S BODY extends horizontally from a vertical pole, rigid as a plank, defying gravity through pure core strength. Nearby, his seventy-one-year-old teammate challenges a man fifty years younger to a push-up contest. Phones rise from the gathering crowd. The young challenger collapses at forty-one. The senior continues, methodical and unfazed, stopping at sixty-four.

Meet Team Strong Silvers: Singapore's fitness enthusiasts turned social media phenomena. Their physiques—washboard abs, vascular arms, gymnastic prowess—have earned them millions of views and a new label: "granfluencers."[1] Beyond their physical capabilities, what's striking about these seniors is how their beliefs about aging fuel behaviors their peers abandoned decades ago—and how those behaviors, in turn, reshape what aging means.

How do our beliefs influence how we age? What if our thoughts affect not only how long we live but also when we die—perhaps even to the day?

Consider a remarkable event that occurred in the summer of 1826.

Thomas Jefferson lay in his bed at Monticello. At eighty-three and bedridden for weeks, he refused to let doctors medicate him into confusion. Instead, he repeatedly asked about the date, expressing his desire to live until the Fourth of July, the fiftieth anniversary of the Declaration of Independence he had authored. When his doctor finally confirmed that it was indeed July 4, Jefferson appeared to take satisfaction in the news. He died at one o'clock that afternoon.[2]

Five hundred miles north in Quincy, Massachusetts, Jefferson's political rival John Adams was also nearing his end. The ninety-year-old's final words, seemingly unaware that Jefferson had already died, were: "Thomas Jefferson survives."[3] He, too, passed away on July 4—remarkably, within hours of Jefferson.

A coincidence? Perhaps. Yet when James Monroe died on July 4, 1831, making him the third president to do so, it suggested something more significant—as if these founding fathers had, in some way, chosen their exit date to align with the nation's birthday. In fact, some medical researchers claim that many people seem to be able to postpone death "until symbolically meaningful occasions."[4]

If our minds can conceivably influence something as profound as the timing of our death, what else might they control? This question takes us deep into the territory of the Second Power of Belief: anticipation.

In the previous chapter, we examined how anticipation influences our subjective experiences, particularly in the context of pain. We saw how expectations alone can activate the brain's "internal pharmacy," releasing natural painkillers that transform our experience of discomfort. It's one thing to say that these anticipation effects change our subjective experience. But do they really influence objective, biological measures of well-being, such as lifespan?

In this chapter, we'll examine claims about mind-body effects that range from scientifically validated to wildly exaggerated. The allure of unlimited mental control over our bodies is undeniably seductive. Who wouldn't want to believe they can think themselves younger, stronger, or healthier? But as we've seen throughout this book, the most liberating beliefs aren't always the most extreme: They're the ones balanced with reality. What follows is a journey to the frontiers of what science knows about the connection between beliefs and biology.

Too Good to Be True

Pop psychology is filled with studies that promise miraculous transformations through the power of thought alone. The stories are compelling, the initial results seem amazing, but the truth is far less magical than the headlines suggest.

In the fall of 1979, a group of elderly men stepped into what felt like a time machine. Their destination wasn't the future but the past—a secluded New England retreat meticulously decorated to look like 1959. Black-and-white television flickered Perry Como, shelves were stacked with 1950s magazines, and even the radios played vintage programs. Every detail had been arranged to create a perfect illusion. For five days, they were instructed not to reminisce, but to behave as if Eisenhower were still president and they were decades younger.

What happened next would launch a thousand dinner party conversations and countless armchair psychologists. The men who had lived "counterclockwise" seemed transformed: sharper memories, better dexterity, and improved hearing. Some observers even thought they looked younger. It was as if believing they were young again had dialed back their biological clocks.

This study, led by Harvard psychologist Ellen Langer,[5] became one of the most captivating stories in the field of mind-body research. It suggested that our mental conception of age might shape our biology.

Other studies carried the same seductive promise. In 2007, another psychology experiment unfolded in hotel corridors. In this study, researchers informed female housekeepers that their daily cleaning routines—vacuuming floors, changing sheets, washing windows—counted as excellent exercise that met the Surgeon General's fitness recommendations.[6] A month later, these women reportedly lost weight, trimmed down their waist-to-hip ratios, and even lowered their blood pressure, all without any changes in their actual work duties or diets. A simple shift in mindset had seemingly melted away fat and improved their health.

Then came the "milkshake study." Volunteers drank the same vanilla milkshake on two occasions, but with different labels. One day, the shake was presented as an indulgent treat made from rich ice cream and labeled "Indulgence—620 calories, high fat, high sugar." On another visit, the very same shake was labeled as a virtuous, diet-friendly drink: "Sensi-shake—140 calories, no added sugar, fat-free."[7] The surprising result? When people believed they'd savored a decadent 620-calorie milkshake, their hunger hormones dropped, as if they'd feasted.

Taken together, these experiments painted a thrilling picture: Maybe the mindsets we adopt could transmute into concrete, biological changes. If elderly men could think themselves younger, if hotel cleaners could shed pounds by viewing their work as exercise, and if perceived calories could manipulate a hunger hormone, what else might be possible?

But here's where the story frays.

For all the fanfare surrounding these studies, they haven't held up well under scientific scrutiny. The experiment involving elderly men was never published in a peer-reviewed scientific journal;[8] its reputation largely rests on popular accounts. Attempts to replicate the housekeeper study failed to show the dramatic changes in weight or body composition initially reported.[9] And the milkshake study's results were far less dramatic than headlines suggested: tiny, inconsistent shifts in hormones, with no differences in actual hunger.

As scientific teams began to poke holes in these mind-over-body marvels, a pattern started to emerge: The more extraordinary the claim, the shakier the evidence and replicability.

It's a seductive idea. Who wouldn't want to believe that changing your mindset about exercise could melt away pounds? Or that immersing yourself in youthful activities could reverse biological aging? But it's also a classic case of wishful thinking—blurring the lines between correlation and causation, between interesting preliminary findings and established facts.

That doesn't mean the mind is powerless over the body. Far from it. The mind does shape the body, but not in the simple, magical way these studies suggest. Belief can spark change, but it travels through deeper, more intricate pathways than mindset alone.

"The Lie Became the Reality"

When Serena Williams was preparing for Wimbledon in 2015, she found herself trapped in a cycle of self-limiting beliefs. Her coach, Patrick Mouratoglou, recalls, "She lost the year before, so she was struggling with her confidence. She was not thinking like Serena."

With only two weeks before the tournament, Mouratoglou realized he needed to intervene—and quickly.[10]

Williams's nerves were especially affecting her play at the net, causing her to hesitate before charging in. "Because she's nervous, she comes to the net and she misses everything. When you're scared to go to the net . . . you're not moving up to get the ball early."

Facing the star's crisis of confidence, and with Wimbledon rapidly approaching, Mouratoglou made a bold decision. He was going to lie. "I come to her," he recounts in his thick French accent, "what I'm going to tell her can be true or not true."

"I have a very good news for you," he told Williams enthusiastically at a strategy session. "Every time you play a match and you create a short ball, I'm super relaxed."

Williams looked surprised. "Why do you say that?"

"Because the stats, it's not me, it's the stats," Mouratoglou replied emphatically. "I know you're going to win 80 percent of the points."

"I thought I sucked at the net," Williams responded, visibly processing.

"Maybe you feel that way," he countered, "but the stats explain exactly the opposite." Mouratoglou anchored the desired behavior in a new belief. "So when there is a short ball, I know you're going to move up, end up at the net," he said, "and win 80 percent of the points. So that's the best news of the day."

In reality, Williams was *not* winning 80 percent of the points at the net. Not even close. But her coach's strategic deception was designed with one purpose: to transform Williams's anticipation of failure into an expectation of success. As Mouratoglou later confessed, "I hate to lie. But as a coach, you have to say the right thing to bring confidence. I lied to Serena about her stats because I knew that if she thought her stats were good, the day after, she would play ten times better."

And that's exactly what happened. When Williams changed her expectations, her performance transformed. "From that day, she was winning 80 percent of the points at the net," he adds with satisfaction. "So the lie became the reality." Williams went on to win the tournament.

Unlike the overblown mindset studies we just examined, Williams's story illustrates something much more tangible. Her coach didn't just change her beliefs; he changed her behavior. Once she believed she would succeed at the net, she approached it more frequently and more confidently. Her physical play underwent a dramatic change, resulting in genuine improvements in her performance.

Williams's story is just one anecdote. However, this pattern—where beliefs change behavior, which then changes outcomes—appears consistently in well-established research on mind-body effects.

In 1972, for instance, an unusual research study unfolded at a Massachusetts gym. Fifteen young men signed up for what they believed was a trial of a new "athletic steroid" designed to increase muscle mass rapidly. The participants, who all had some weightlifting experience but weren't competitive bodybuilders, were eager to experience the dramatic gains promised by this supposedly breakthrough compound.

They took their pills diligently for four weeks while continuing their regular workout routines. By the end of the month, the results were striking. On a wide range of lifts—bench press, military press, squat, clean and jerk—these men improved their performance much more than members of a control group who received no intervention. Their bench press strength increased by an impressive twenty-nine pounds in just a month. It looked exactly like what they'd been promised.[11]

There was just one twist: The "athletic steroid" they'd been taking was nothing more than a placebo. The capsules contained zero active ingredients—no anabolic compounds, no hormones, nothing that could have directly stimulated muscle growth. Yet these men had built measurable strength simply because they believed they were taking steroids.

Unlike many of the mind-body studies we discussed earlier in the chapter, this placebo steroid study has stood the test of time. Replications have found the same result: Participants gained strength from placebo steroids.[12] The takeaway is clear: Anticipation can lead to measurable improvements in physical performance and even body composition.

But how do fake pills build muscle? If the "steroids" contained no active ingredient, what mechanism could explain these genuine physical changes?

The answer doesn't lie in some mystical mind-over-matter force; it lies in something much more straightforward: motivation and effort. The men who believed they were taking steroids most likely approached their workouts differently. The factors at play were the same ones that help any of us excel in the gym: training with greater intensity, pushing to complete more repetitions, and attempting heavier weights. Believing that they had pharmaceutical assistance made them anticipate success, which translated directly into behavioral changes. They simply tried harder.

This doesn't mean the placebo effect wasn't "real"—it was. The strength gains were measurable and significant. But understanding the mechanism matters. These placebos worked primarily by changing behavior, rather than by directly altering physiology through thought alone.

Recall that motivation requires three elements: belief (the conviction that something is possible), behavior (the actions taken), and benefit (the reward). The placebo steroid study illustrates the Motivation Triangle in action, with anticipation serving as the crucial bridge that turns belief into behavior.

The men's belief that they were taking performance-enhancing drugs created an anticipation of success, which drove behavioral changes (increased training effort), which ultimately produced genuine benefits (increased strength). The anticipation wasn't magical—it was motivational.

A growing body of research demonstrates that strategic deception can also boost cognitive capabilities and creative problem-solving. In one study, participants were asked to smell a neutral substance. However, for some, the researchers assigned a label, calling it a "creativity-enhancing" aroma. Those who believed they were breathing in a creativity-boosting scent subsequently performed significantly better on standardized tests for out-of-the-box thinking than a control group that smelled the same neutral odor but was not informed about its effects.[13]

In another experiment, participants received what they thought was noninvasive brain stimulation during a learning task. The placebo group believed their brains were being stimulated by a mild electrical current, though no stimulation was occurring, and were told this would enhance their mental performance. These participants showed greater accuracy and faster reaction times than members of a control group who were not led to expect any enhancement.[14]

When you expect improved performance, your brain responds

by enhancing attention, reducing performance anxiety, and often increasing effort—all of which contribute to genuinely better outcomes. The placebo works not by bypassing biology, but by triggering it.

The Experience Loop (Believe-Anticipate-Feel-Confirm), which we explored in chapters 5 and 6, provides a helpful framework for understanding these phenomena. Consider the men in the steroid study. They

- *believed* they were taking effective performance enhancers,
- *anticipated* improved strength and muscle gains,
- *felt* empowered to push harder in their workouts, and
- *confirmed* their expectations when they observed real improvements.

This positive feedback loop amplified the initial belief, creating a virtuous cycle of improvement. They didn't just think differently. Their new thoughts altered their behavior, resulting in objectively measurable physical changes.

The key insight here is that placebos work by unlocking motivation, directing attention, and triggering natural physiological responses. Our expectations genuinely shape our capabilities, often in ways that exceed our imagination. However, activating this potential requires more than just belief alone.

Revealing Hidden Potential

"Crocodile! Crocodile!" rang through the sleep laboratory in the middle of the night, startling the observers on duty. A Parkinson's patient, who normally struggled to speak even a few soft words, was now bellowing at the top of his lungs. According to Dr. Isabelle Arnulf, a professor of neurology at the Sorbonne in Paris, "The patient had been dreaming of crocodiles in the sleep lab when he lifted a heavy bedside table above his head and loudly shouted." During his waking hours, the patient could barely lift everyday objects. Now, he was fending off imaginary reptiles with furniture.[15]

This observation—that a person could perform physical feats while asleep that they found impossible while awake—tells us something important about human capability. Our bodies often possess potential that remains locked away by our brains. In the Parkinson's patient's case, his conscious limitations were temporarily suspended during sleep, and his body revealed what it was actually capable of doing.

What we can see here is a further dimension of anticipation effects. Sometimes our beliefs don't just make us try harder; they remove barriers to capabilities we already possess but cannot access.

Consider the nuns and monks of Eastern Tibet. As dawn breaks over monasteries encased in frost and snow, they sit in unheated stone chambers, where temperatures plummet to well below freezing. Yet these clergy meditate wearing nothing but thin cotton sheets. While others would succumb to hypothermia, they use a practice known as *g-tummo* to remain not just alive but remarkably warm. Their skin actually radiates heat that melts the frost around them.[16] While ordinary humans shiver helplessly in the cold, these meditation masters transform their bodies into living furnaces. During what's known as forceful breath meditation, practitioners were observed in a 2013 study to generate internal heat, raising their core temperature to a moderate fever zone (up to 38.3° Celsius)—a biological feat that control subjects, despite their best efforts to mimic the techniques, could not replicate.[17]

Among the many things that make this ability remarkable, the most important is that it involves intentional regulation of what we typically consider "automatic" or involuntary bodily functions—processes supposedly beyond conscious control. The g-tummo practitioners demonstrate that this is not always the case: Through specific anticipatory practices, they access capabilities that most people never realize they possess.

Researchers at Harvard have identified specific neurons near the base of the brain that can partially explain the Tibetan meditators' abilities. Contrary to common belief, fever is not directly caused by an infection itself; rather, the brain deliberately raises body temperature to create an inhospitable environment for pathogens. The Harvard researchers discovered an area within the hypothalamus that can directly trigger fever and other sickness mechanisms.[18]

So if you've ever had a fever, you have this power too—you just don't know how to use it. What makes these Tibetan practitioners exceptional is their apparent ability to access and activate these neurological mechanisms voluntarily, without the presence of sickness. Through their meditation techniques, they've developed the rare capacity to communicate with neural pathways normally reserved for immune response, effectively commanding their bodies to generate heat at will. Far from being a supernatural ability, it is, in fact, an extraordinary degree of control over natural biological systems through the power of belief.

The secret lies in a symphony of body and mind—specialized breathing techniques called *vase breathing*, in which practitioners hold their breath while tensing abdominal muscles, combined with vivid mental visualizations of inner fire. As the clergy's minds focus intensely on images of flames rising through their spines, they anticipate warmth and ignite thermogenesis processes that are likely dormant in ordinary humans.

We can see the same pattern—beliefs unlocking surprising latent capabilities—in many other contexts. Perhaps one of the most revealing studies along these lines involved sleep perception. Researchers connected participants to various monitoring devices and then gave them false feedback about the quality of their sleep. Some were told they had experienced above-average REM sleep quality (deep, high-quality sleep), while others were told their sleep quality was below average. All of these shared findings were based on fake EEG readings. Despite no actual differences in their sleep, those who were told they had superior sleep subsequently performed better on cognitive tests of addition and word association than those told their sleep quality was poor. The belief that they had slept well unlocked a higher level of performance.[19]

What's particularly noteworthy is that the differences weren't just in subjective measures, such as self-reported alertness, but also in objective cognitive tests. The participants' anticipation of performing well, given their well-rested state, led to measurable improvements in their results.

Athletic performance provides numerous examples of anticipation unlocking previously hidden capabilities. In a 2009 study, scientists asked cyclists to pedal to exhaustion while watching a clock that showed their elapsed time. Unknown to the participants, researchers had secretly modified the clocks to run either faster or slower than usual. When the clocks ran slow (making cyclists think they hadn't been exercising as long as they actually had), they persisted significantly longer before exhaustion. Their bodies were capable of more—they just needed the right anticipation to access that potential.[20]

Similarly, a 2012 study found that cyclists, when falsely told they were pedaling more slowly than their actual speed, were able to maintain faster speeds with no increase in perceived exertion. Their anticipation of a manageable pace allowed them to perform better than they typically could.[21]

All these examples demonstrate a common point: When psychological constraints are removed or altered, anticipation can reveal capabilities we don't know we possess, leading to fundamental shifts in what our bodies can accomplish.

The Biology of Belief

Let's return to Team Strong Silvers, the senior fitness enthusiasts from Singapore we met at the beginning of this chapter. Their rejection of conventional beliefs about aging has led them to maintain training routines that most people their age gave up long ago. Are they simply unusual individuals, or do they represent something more profound about how beliefs shape the aging process?

Dr. Becca Levy at Yale University has led groundbreaking research on precisely this question. In a landmark longitudinal study, Levy and colleagues followed 660 people aged fifty and older for nearly twenty-three years. They discovered that those with more positive views of aging lived, on average, 7.5 years longer than those with negative views, even after controlling for health status, socioeconomic factors, and other variables.[22]

This wasn't a minor statistical blip. The impact of positive aging beliefs on longevity was greater than the effects of lower blood pressure or cholesterol (which add about four years), or maintaining a healthy weight, not smoking, and exercising regularly (which add about one to three years each). When researchers measured biomarkers of aging, they found that positive beliefs were associated with healthier profiles, including lower inflammation markers and stress hormones. But again, these biological differences weren't magical; they emerged from concrete behavioral and psychological pathways.

What do these pathways look like, and how do beliefs about aging affect them? Here's an example: When people hold negative aging beliefs ("I might fall" or "I'm too old for this"), they're more likely to avoid physical challenges. Avoiding challenges leads, over time, to actual physical deconditioning. The deconditioning makes activities more difficult and potentially more painful, which reinforces avoidance. Socially, this often leads to isolation, which increases stress and depression risk. The resulting chronic stress triggers inflammatory responses and disrupts hormone regulation, accelerating biological aging in measurable ways.

Team Strong Silvers demonstrates the opposite cycle. Their belief in continued adaptation and growth leads them to train harder (behavior). These workouts build actual physical strength and capability (biology), which reduces injury concerns (psychology) and encourages more training and involvement with their fitness community (social behavior). That, in turn, reduces inflammatory responses and stress hormones (biology), reinforcing their improved health and validating the initial positive beliefs that started the cycle.

Intervention studies demonstrate this positive cycle at work. For example, when older adults are exposed to positive messages about aging, they immediately perform better on physical tests such as walking speed.[23] These temporary shifts in expectations can lead to immediate behavioral changes: Participants try harder and move differently when freed from limiting age expectations.

Levy's research has consistently shown that how we think about aging affects how we age. The effects operate through multiple pathways:

- **Cognitive functioning:** People with positive aging beliefs show better memory performance and slower cognitive decline compared to those with negative views.[24]
- **Cardiovascular health:** They exhibit better cardiovascular stress responses, with lower blood pressure and heart rate increases during challenging tasks.[25]
- **Recovery from disability:** Following disabling health events, they recover functional abilities more fully and quickly than those with negative beliefs.[26]
- **Preventive health behaviors:** They are more likely to engage in preventive health measures like regular exercise, proper nutrition, and medication adherence.[27]

But perhaps most remarkable is how early these age beliefs form and how long their effects persist. In one study, Levy found that stereotypes about aging absorbed in early life predicted cardiovascular events up to thirty-eight years later. Participants who had held more negative age stereotypes in young adulthood were significantly more likely to experience heart attacks or strokes in later life than those with more positive views, even after accounting for other risk factors.[28]

This means that the stories we tell ourselves about aging matter far more than we may think. When a culture bombards people with messages equating aging with inevitable decline, helplessness, and irrelevance, those messages manifest in physical reality. The belief that "I'm too old for this" might seem like a reasonable assessment of reality, but it's a terrible way to live. Conversely, the belief that "My body can thrive at any age" may seem optimistically biased, but it's an excellent tool that drives behaviors that create measurable biological benefits.

Aging is inevitable. But how our bodies experience the passage of time is substantially influenced by the beliefs that drive our actions.

The Reality of Our Beliefs

Throughout this chapter, we've seen how beliefs shape biology through concrete physiological and behavioral pathways. When we embrace the belief that our bodies are capable of continued adaptation, we act differently. Unlike genetic factors or past exposures, our beliefs remain malleable throughout our lives. By deliberately cultivating beliefs that promote improvement rather than limitation, we can influence our bodily experiences.

The beliefs we hold about aging itself may be the most consequential of all. As years pass, these assumptions gain increasing power. Will we anticipate continual vitality or inevitable decline? Will we interpret physical changes as signals to evolve or reasons to withdraw? Will we see ourselves as active contributors to our health or diminished bystanders?

These questions matter because beliefs shape behavior, and behavior, in turn, shapes biology. The extraordinary physical feats of the

Strong Silvers aren't miracles. They're the natural result of expecting capability to persist, training consistently based on that expectation, and letting biology respond accordingly.

Our bodies don't just contain beliefs. They respond to them, continually reshaping in harmony with what we expect. Understanding this relationship transforms aging from something that happens to us into something we actively navigate, not with naive optimism or resigned fatalism, but with informed agency over how we live each stage of life.

FROM LIMITING BELIEFS...	TO LIBERATING BELIEFS...
Getting older means inevitable decline and limitation.	My body is capable of continued adaptation at any stage of life.
My current physical performance reflects my potential.	My body likely possesses capabilities I haven't yet accessed.
Avoiding challenges protects me from injury or failure.	Embracing appropriate challenges builds strength and reveals what I'm capable of.
I'm too old/young/weak to try that activity.	Age and current ability are starting points, not permanent limitations.
If I feel tired or sluggish, that's just how I am.	My feelings often reflect my expectations and can change with my mindset.

Important Note

You've learned that beliefs shape not only what you see but also what you feel. To help you turn this knowledge into lasting change, I've created bonus resources with reflection guides and exercises that train you to reset expectations, unlock hidden potential, and elevate your everyday life.

Go to NirAndFar.com/belief-tools/ or scan the QR code below.

THE THIRD POWER OF BELIEF

AGENCY

The
Power to
DO
What You
Believe

*You can't climb the ladder of success with
your hands in your pockets.*
—ARNOLD SCHWARZENEGGER

CHAPTER 8

How to Take Control of Your Life (Even When It's Impossible)

Believe you have control, even when you don't.

THE SOUND THAT terrifies every musher isn't the howl of wolves or the crack of breaking ice. It's the subtle snap of a tether followed by silence. In that instant, your entire world changes. Your dog team has broken free and is racing away, taking your supplies, shelter, and survival with them. This was Blair Braverman's nightmare as she navigated the treacherous Alaskan wilderness during the Iditarod, the world's most demanding sled dog race. "People have this idea that the dogs will wait for you. But in fact, they will just be happier [without you]," she explains.[1]

In dog sledding, as in life, there are no guarantees. No promise that things will go according to plan. No assurance that the world will accommodate your needs or wait while you catch up. Survival depends on one thing: hanging on when everything inside you screams to let go.

The question Braverman faced—the same question we all face in our lives—wasn't whether chaos would appear, but how to respond when it did. This question strikes at the heart of human existence:

Do we truly have control over our lives? Or are we merely passengers, carried along by forces beyond our influence?

In the previous chapters, we explored the first two powers of belief. The power of attention demonstrates how beliefs influence what we see, while the power of anticipation reveals how beliefs shape what we feel. Now we turn to the third and perhaps most transformative power, agency: the power to *do* what we believe. This is the ultimate expression of belief's influence on our lives, where our internal convictions translate into external action.

This capacity for agency—this ability to act rather than merely be acted upon—turns out to be far more counterintuitive than scientists once thought. The latest neuroscience has exposed a startling truth about how our sense of control actually works in the brain— findings that overturn decades of accepted wisdom. These discoveries suggest that the path to the life we want requires a fundamental shift in how we think about the notion of control.

The Dogs That Wouldn't Quit

In the late 1960s, behavioral scientists Martin Seligman and Steven Maier conducted a series of experiments that would revolutionize our understanding of human psychology. They placed dogs in small hammocks and subjected them to mild electric shocks under one of two conditions. Some dogs could press a panel with their nose to stop the shocks, while for the other dogs, pressing the panel did nothing.[2]

The next day, the dogs were placed in a shuttle box where they were supposed to learn to escape the shock on one side by simply jumping over a low barrier to the other. The researchers anticipated that the previous day's conditioning would accelerate learning. Instead, something unexpected happened. Dogs that had learned to stop the shocks quickly escaped, but those that had endured inescapable zaps didn't even try. They lay down and whimpered, as if they had concluded that nothing they did would make any difference.[3]

Seligman and Maier termed this behavior *learned helplessness*. Their theory suggests that when animals or humans experience enough uncontrollable bad events, they learn that nothing they do matters. This learning carries over into new situations, causing them to give up even when escape becomes possible. This insight transformed our understanding of depression, trauma, and resilience, spawning thousands of studies and influencing treatment approaches worldwide.

However, a detail buried in their data haunted the researchers for decades: A few of the dogs never gave up, no matter how many uncontrollable shocks they endured. These animals appeared to be immune to learned helplessness.

This oddity contained a clue to an essential truth about human motivation that would take over fifty years to explain. Only with the invention of modern brain imaging technology did Maier discover that helplessness, in fact, isn't learned at all—a stunning reversal of the original theory of learned helplessness.[4]

Peering into the brain's neural circuitry, Maier observed that when the brain encounters an uncontrollable situation, it first triggers an automatic freeze response. But when an animal believes it may have a chance, another brain region is activated. The ventromedial prefrontal cortex detects hope and actively inhibits the passive response.

Remember the swimming rats from Richter's study? Those who were saved and then returned to the cylinders swam for days, while the others gave up and drowned within minutes. Similarly, the dogs that wouldn't quit likely had prior experiences where escape proved successful, allowing them to draw upon a learned response to override their instinctive passivity.

This discovery suggests something profound about human nature. Helplessness isn't learned at all. It's our default. What we must learn is hope.

These neural circuits are strengthened through experience. Each time you successfully exert control in a challenging situation, you reinforce the brain pathways that can override your passive defaults—and activate what Seligman calls your "hope circuit."[5] Over time, this creates what amounts to a new operating system for dealing with adversity, one that views problems not as threats to avoid but as challenges to engage.

Research confirms that we can deliberately strengthen our control circuitry through what psychologists refer to as *mastery experiences*. One particularly striking example comes from research on the treatment of phobias. In a study at Northwestern University, participants with severe arachnophobia underwent a single two-hour session involving progressively closer contact with a live tarantula. By the end of the session, all of the participants were able to touch or hold the spider—something they had previously considered impossible to do. Brain scans revealed changes in their neural wiring, specifically in regions involved in emotion regulation and fear processing, after just this brief intervention.[6]

Similar results appear across domains, from public speaking anxiety to post-traumatic stress. The key lies in building neural pathways that allow effective action despite fear or discomfort. This explains why exposure therapy is among the most effective treatments for anxiety. Rather than attempting to eliminate anxiety directly, it builds evidence of your capacity to function effectively even while anxious.[7]

Understanding this neurological foundation changes everything we thought we knew about motivation, resilience, and personal change. It explains why positive thinking alone so often fails to create lasting transformation. Simply telling yourself you have control isn't enough. Your brain needs direct evidence that change is possible. Every small victory that proves our actions matter helps build beliefs that override our default passivity.

Think about what this means for your own life. Those moments when you feel stuck—procrastinating on an important project, delaying a significant financial decision, hesitating to make a career change— aren't evidence of personal failure. They're your brain's ancient cognitive system doing precisely what it evolved to do: defaulting to fear and helplessness in the face of uncertain outcomes.

But you're not trapped. You can train your brain to override passivity and reclaim agency. What you need are targeted moments of control: small wins that prove to your mind that your actions matter, that change is possible, and that you are not helpless.

Fighting Chaos

When Blair Braverman first stepped on the runners ten years before the Iditarod, she had a very different mindset about what was in her control. She recalled, "I dreamed of one clean run. A run where nothing went wrong."[8] Every tangle in the lines, every unexpected weather shift, every dog that wouldn't listen felt like evidence of her inadequacy, proof that she wasn't cut out for the challenge.

Most of us operate from a similar mindset. When our task list overflows, when a project starts showing signs of failure, when relationships become complicated, we interpret these challenges as personal shortcomings. We see chaos as an indictment of our capabilities rather than a natural part of life.

Over time, Braverman's beliefs transformed. "I had stopped seeing problems, even dangerous ones, as disasters and started seeing them as a normal part of travel in deep wilderness." This shift from seeing chaos as the enemy to seeing it as the terrain changed how she approached each challenge.

When she approached The Steps—three near-vertical drops that struck fear into even experienced mushers—her body flooded with biochemical signals urging her to stop. One mistake could send the sled, dogs, and musher tumbling hundreds of feet down to the frozen river below. Years of training had built more than skill—they had forged a belief in her own agency, the conviction that she could act decisively even in extreme circumstances. She no longer wished for an easy run; she trusted her ability to navigate whatever came her way.

What if chaos isn't evidence of our shortcomings, but proof of something else entirely?

In 1944, physicist Erwin Schrödinger posed what seems like a child's question: What makes something alive? Not in a spiritual sense, but physically. What fundamental property separates living things from dead matter?

Schrödinger concluded that living things wage a constant battle against entropy—that relentless force pulling the universe toward disorder.[9] While mountains erode to dust, stars burn out their fuel and collapse, and even black holes slowly dissolve into radiation, life stands defiantly against this cosmic current. In every cell, in every organism, in every ecosystem, living things build islands of intricate order in an ocean of increasing chaos.

A seed breaks through earth to reach sunlight. A honeybee colony converts random nectar gatherings into wax to form perfectly hexagonal combs of mathematical precision. A coral reef arranges millions of tiny polyps into vast underwater cities of color and complexity. This is life's signature: not just surviving disorder but actively creating order from it.

Think about your own body. Right now, trillions of cells are orchestrating an intricate dance, maintaining precise temperature controls, repairing microscopic damage, and transforming simple molecules into usable energy.[10] Every breath defies entropy. Every heartbeat is a rebellion. Every cellular response represents a tiny victory against decay. Eventually, when we die, our bodies return to stardust—the inevitable defeat of life's 3.8-billion-year battle that sparked your existence.

To paraphrase Schrödinger, life is that which fights chaos. This perspective transforms how we might view our daily struggles. When your life feels chaotic, remember: Disorder isn't a sign that you're failing at life; it's proof that you're fully immersed in it. If things feel messy, it's because you're alive, and that's an improbable, beautiful miracle. The goal isn't to eliminate disorder (that's impossible); rather, it is to develop a productive relationship with it.

This perspective on life as an active battle against chaos directly connects to the power of agency. Just as your body fights entropy at the cellular level, your mind can develop beliefs that help you navigate life's inevitable disorder. Agency doesn't mean controlling every variable. It means developing beliefs that support effective navigation of uncertainty. As with attention and anticipation, agency beliefs don't rely on absolute truth. Braverman had no certainty she would finish the Iditarod alive. What she had were beliefs that made her more effective in the face of the challenges at hand.

This is the critical distinction between high and low agency. Someone with low agency sees obstacles as immovable barriers that signal, "Stop" (like the dogs that whimpered and gave up). Someone with high agency sees those same obstacles as navigation points that signal, "Adapt."

Those with high agency don't naively expect fewer problems. Instead, they trust in their ability to respond effectively to whatever issues might arise. The focus shifts from "How can I avoid difficulty?" to "How can I handle difficulty when it inevitably appears?"

The Man Who Moved a Mountain

Sometimes an individual's belief in their capacity for action becomes so powerful that it reshapes not just their own neural pathways but the physical world itself.

On a scorching morning in 1960, a laborer named Dashrath Manjhi picked up a hammer and chisel and walked to the base of a mountain in the remote village of Gehlaur, India. Manjhi was a member of the Musahar caste, among the most marginalized and impoverished in Indian society—landless workers traditionally relegated to catching and eating rats for survival.

Villagers watched this slight man, barely five feet tall, raise his hammer against the massive wall of rock. The first strike echoed through the valley. Then another. And another.

The villagers shook their heads, wondering if grief had finally broken him.

A year earlier, Manjhi's pregnant wife, Falguni Devi, had fallen and sustained severe injuries while traversing a mountain path. The nearest doctor was less than a mile away, but the mountain forced villagers to take a circuitous route of roughly forty miles to reach medical care. For Devi, it was too late.[11]

Standing over her body, Manjhi made a decision. The mountain had to go.

Every morning before dawn, he made his way to the rock face. Each evening, after long hours in the fields, he came back again. The labor was brutal. The stone was quartzite, among the hardest on Earth. His tools were meager: a hammer and a rough iron chisel. In the searing heat of summer, the rock scorched his hands; in the monsoons, the surface turned slick and treacherous.

For the first few years, progress seemed invisible. Still, Manjhi kept hammering—strike by strike, chip by chip, until the rock began to yield. After five years, he carved a shallow depression. After ten, a visible groove. He sold his goats to buy better tools and worked through injuries. He tried pleading with the government to help, but schemes collapsed and promises dissolved. Villagers called him insane, dubbing him the village idiot for attempting the impossible. His own family pleaded with him to abandon the seemingly futile task.

But Manjhi didn't quit. Gradually, villagers who once mocked him began supporting his mission, providing food, water, and tools.

By 1982, after twenty-two years of solitary labor, Dashrath Manjhi had carved a passage approximately 360 feet long, 30 feet wide, and 25 feet deep through solid rock. The journey, which once required a detour of over forty miles, was shortened dramatically to just nine. Children could now easily reach schools. Farmers gained efficient access to markets. The sick could reach hospitals in time.

Manjhi's story illustrates what so often separates those who persist from those who don't: his belief in his power to make a difference. Psychologists call this the *locus of control*.[12] Individuals with an external locus believe that power over their lives resides with fate, luck, or others. Those with an internal locus of control see themselves as agents capable of influencing outcomes through their actions.

Manjhi exemplified this internal locus. He couldn't revive his wife, compel governmental action, or alter his caste. But he could pick up a hammer and break rock. And so he did, day after day, decade after decade, proving that even the most immovable obstacles yield, eventually, to those who keep swinging.

Agency Works

Manjhi's most significant legacy isn't the changes to his town's roads but the lasting proof that individual agency can triumph over seemingly insurmountable barriers. While his circumstances were extraordinary, research confirms that his approach of maintaining belief in personal agency despite external constraints consistently produces superior outcomes across nearly every area of life.

Mental Health: Control beliefs predict psychological well-being across cultures. Those with an internal locus of control experience lower rates of depression and anxiety, recover more quickly from trauma, and report higher levels of life satisfaction and purpose—effects that persist even when controlling for actual circumstances. A study that compared Holocaust survivors decades after their liberation found that those who had maintained a sense of internal control during imprisonment (often through small acts of mental or interpersonal agency) showed significantly lower rates of post-traumatic stress symptoms compared to those who had adopted a more external orientation.[13]

Physical Health: Individuals with a stronger internal locus of control exhibit better health outcomes across multiple measures. They experience lower rates of chronic illness, recover more quickly from disease and injury, and demonstrate stronger immune function in laboratory tests.[14] One particularly striking study tracked approximately 7,500 British children into adulthood and found that those with a strong internal locus of control at age ten were significantly less likely to report poor health as adults.[15]

Relationships: Those with an internal locus of control tend to have more satisfying and resilient relationships. When conflicts occur, they are more likely to address issues directly rather than waiting for their partner or circumstances to change. Individuals with strong internal control beliefs also maintain more supportive relationships during significant life transitions.[16] Rather than simply reacting to life changes, they actively invest in key relationships, creating a reinforcing cycle: A sense of personal agency strengthens social ties and those ties help sustain agency during tough times.[17]

Professional Success: An internal locus consistently predicts higher income and is associated with faster career advancement and greater job satisfaction across various industries. A twenty-two-year longitudinal study found that locus of control measured in adolescence significantly predicted adult income, alongside IQ, parental socioeconomic status, and academic achievement.[18] Other research also confirms this pattern in entrepreneurship, predicting greater business growth, life satisfaction, and sustainable entrepreneurial endeavors.[19]

The pattern is unmistakable: Maintaining a strong internal locus of control consistently predicts better outcomes, even when objective analysis suggests you lack control. This overturns the idea that action is only worthwhile when conditions are favorable. See the constraints clearly, then focus relentlessly on what you can influence.

Research reveals that agency beliefs operate as a fundamental lens shaping how we experience life itself. They transform how we interpret, respond to, and ultimately experience everything that happens to us. Consider what this means in practical terms: Someone facing workplace discrimination, health challenges, or economic hardship who focuses exclusively on external forces typically experiences worse outcomes than someone who maintains agency beliefs while acknowledging those same realities. The objective circumstances remain identical. The difference lies in where the individual directs their attention and energy.

Education reform offers a compelling example. One study found that teaching students that intelligence can be developed through effort (an agency belief) produced meaningful improvements in academic performance, particularly among economically disadvantaged students.[20] Systemic reform still matters, but this finding reveals something often overlooked: Within even the most imperfect systems, agency beliefs can spark meaningful change.

Yet agency has its limits. Taken too far, it slips into the trap of *naive omnipotence*—the belief that sheer effort can bend any circumstance to your will. Research shows that those who ignore genuine constraints often end up frustrated, burned out, and disillusioned. Research from places like Japan and China suggests a more effective approach: Individuals who combine personal initiative with an acknowledgment of external forces, such as community and family, prove more resilient than those who cling to total self-determination.[21]

Healthy agency beliefs begin by recognizing reality clearly and end with acting, often relentlessly, where your actions matter most. This is what both Dashrath Manjhi and Blair Braverman discovered. Every morning, Manjhi faced the same choice: Surrender to circumstances or strike the stone again. He chose the hammer. Braverman couldn't control the weather, the trail conditions, or her dogs' instincts, but she could control her preparation, decisions, focus, and interpretation of challenges. By directing attention to their true spheres of influence, each transformed their view of obstacles from a state of helplessness into determined action.

Building Your Agency

Twenty hours into a storm during the Iditarod, Blair Braverman sat alone in a shelter cabin, dangerously low on dog food. If she ran out, the race was over. The old default would have been to quit.

Instead, she radioed a race judge, who told her there was a small group of mushers ahead. If she could catch them, they might be able to spare some supplies. So she pushed through whiteout conditions for three hours, chasing the faint hope of help. When she finally reached the group, a musher named Victoria greeted her with thirty pounds of dog food—more than enough to keep going.[22]

"We got this crazy second chance," Braverman later reflected. The next time she saw lights on the horizon, they were the lights of Nome—the finish line.

This moment captures a crucial truth about agency: Agency doesn't mean having all the answers yourself. It means believing in your ability to find solutions and staying committed until you do. Braverman's journey from novice to Iditarod finisher offers a blueprint for cultivating agency in your own life, whether you're facing a challenging work project, a difficult relationship, health concerns, or simply the daily chaos of modern existence. And like Braverman, you can train that capacity. Research points to specific practices that, taken together, reinforce the belief that your actions matter.

START WITH EVIDENCE

Each time you take on a challenge just beyond your comfort zone and succeed, you give your brain undeniable proof that your actions shape outcomes. Psychologists refer to these as *optimal challenges*. Even small wins—such as a daily ten-minute walk when strenuous exercise feels too overwhelming—can train your brain to believe that effort matters.

I've seen this in my own life. My public speaking career didn't begin with a TED Talk. It started much smaller—an audience of a few dozen people. Initially, the idea of presenting to a crowd of strangers seemed daunting. But communicating ideas I cared about was a thrill that gave me tangible proof I could do it. Each opportunity built on the last—larger audiences, higher stakes, more substantial evidence that I could meet the challenge.

FOCUS WHERE IT COUNTS

Agency grows when you direct effort where you have leverage. Resilient people distinguish among what they can control, what they can influence, and what lies beyond their reach. In studies of ICU nurses, the most resilient weren't the ones trying to control every variable. They were the ones who adapted—stepping in when needed, collaborating with colleagues, deferring to specialists, and accepting outcomes they couldn't change. Researchers call this adaptability *control flexibility*.[23] Agency doesn't mean controlling everything. It means knowing where your effort matters most.

SHAPE THE STORY YOU TELL YOURSELF

Setbacks aren't defined only by what happens but also by how you explain them: permanent vs. temporary, global vs. specific, personal vs. circumstantial. Resilient individuals construct narratives that highlight their ability to take action, even in the face of hardship, and these stories reinforce both identity and action.[24]

Few embodied this more clearly than Anthony Ray Hinton, who spent nearly thirty years on death row for crimes he did not commit. His wrongful conviction and years in solitary confinement could have crushed him, but Hinton refused to let others write his story. "They stole my 30s, they stole my 40s, they stole my 50s," he recalled. "I could not afford to give them my soul. I couldn't give them me."

Humor became one of the tools he used—cracking jokes with guards, teasing fellow inmates, reminding everyone, including himself, that he was still human. But the deeper anchor was the narrative he chose: that even in the most dehumanizing conditions, he retained agency over his identity. His agency carried him through confinement—and eventually to his exoneration—and fuels his advocacy today.[25]

BUILD SYSTEMS THAT CARRY YOU

Sometimes the most effective way to strengthen agency is to reduce reliance on willpower. Systems and routines make consistent action the default. Blair Braverman's strict schedules for feeding and resting her dogs carried her through exhaustion and storms on the Iditarod trail. Research on habit formation confirms why this works: External structures make progress possible even when confidence or energy is running low.[26] The key is to design systems in calm moments so they'll sustain you in chaotic ones. Then the cycle repeats: Systems generate new evidence, evidence sharpens focus, focus strengthens the story, and the story supports systems. Step by step, belief compounds—until agency becomes self-perpetuating.

The Choice Is Yours

The world can feel overwhelmingly chaotic. The alarming headlines we consume daily can form a relentless wave of uncertainty, nudging the brain toward its passive default. It's no wonder so many people report feeling helpless, overwhelmed, or stuck.

But the answer isn't less chaos; it's more agency. The path forward lies not in somehow making the world more predictable, but in building our capacity to navigate the unpredictable. Like Blair Braverman taming The Steps, you can transform your relationship with doubt itself.

That is the ultimate promise of the Third Power of Belief: the power to do what you believe. Not because challenges disappear, but because you develop the capacity to meet them effectively. Not because you gain control over everything, but because you learn to direct your energy where it matters most.

The sled is before you. The trail stretches ahead, full of uncertainty and challenge. Will you wait for perfect conditions or build the agency to navigate whatever may come? Will you focus on what's beyond your control or direct your energy where it can make a difference?

The trail awaits. The choice is yours.

FROM LIMITING BELIEFS...	TO LIBERATING BELIEFS...
I tend to focus on what's wrong with the situation.	I can focus relentlessly on what I can control.
Feeling helpless means I am helpless.	Helplessness is my brain's default—agency must be learned.
I need ideal conditions before taking action.	I can navigate uncertainty and act despite chaos.
If I can't control everything, why try anything?	I can influence outcomes within my sphere of control.
Past challenges or failures predict future outcomes.	Each setback teaches me how to respond more effectively.

CHAPTER 9

Prayer Works, With or Without Faith

Ritual is the bridge to your better self.

WHEN I WAS six years old, I talked to God.

My family was in crisis. My parents had been scammed out of nearly every penny they had, with no hope of getting their money back. Facing financial ruin, their arguments escalated to screaming matches that shook our house. Even forty years later, I can still hear those echoes.

To escape, I developed a ritual. Each morning, before anyone else was awake, I slipped outside to our concrete driveway, lay on my back, and gazed up at the fading stars. That was when I spoke to God.

I called Him by name. The voice that responded wasn't audible, yet it felt distinct from my own thoughts: calmer, wiser, more reassuring. As I poured out my fears, this presence told me that despite the chaos unfolding at home, I would be okay. My family would find its way through this mess. I wasn't alone.

Those early morning conversations became my sanctuary. But somewhere along the path to adulthood, the connection faded. As I developed a more rational, evidence-based worldview, prayer began to feel strange—if I couldn't prove that anyone was listening, wasn't I just talking to myself? What had once brought comfort now seemed suspect, tainted by what I perceived as magical thinking. This shift wasn't sudden; the connection faded like a 1980s Polaroid of my youth left too long in the sun.

By adulthood, prayer was a distant memory, shelved alongside other abandoned childhood fantasies. Yet I couldn't shake the sense that something valuable had been left behind. Decades later, research pulled me back to the practice I had dismissed.

What does science reveal about the power of prayer? Can we experience its benefits without certainty about God? And what do ancient religious traditions and cutting-edge research alike teach us about how to pray and what to pray for?

Power from Prayer

When I returned to the question of prayer, I expected little more than platitudes and comforting words. What I discovered instead was a wealth of research. Far from being dismissed as mere superstition, prayer leaves measurable fingerprints on the brain and body.

Researchers at Columbia University found that people who valued spirituality had measurably thicker cerebral cortices—the brain region that typically thins in individuals suffering from depression.[1] Over two decades of follow-up, spirituality proved remarkably protective: a 75 percent reduction in depression, rising to nearly 90 percent for those most prone to it.

Other studies tell a similar story, revealing prayer's link to calmer physiology and significantly lower reactivity of cortisol, the body's primary stress hormone.[2] Across dozens of studies, religious practice correlates with lower rates of anxiety, substance abuse, and overall mortality. While factors like social support may contribute to these outcomes, controlled studies suggest that prayer itself provides independent benefits.

Brain scans add another layer of understanding. People who pray regularly exhibit increased gray matter in regions associated with emotional regulation, self-control, and compassion. In daily life, these changes translate into increased patience in the face of frustration and greater endurance in the face of life's inevitable challenges.[3]

Consider this groundbreaking experiment. In a brightly lit laboratory, buckets of near-freezing water chilled the air as eighty-four college students shuffled nervously, awaiting instructions. The challenge was deceptively simple yet daunting: Immerse a hand in the icy water and hold it there until the pain became unbearable.

Weeks earlier, each student had been trained in one of three coping methods. One group practiced basic physical relaxation techniques. Another group meditated using secular, neutral phrases such as "I am content" or "I am joyful." The third group recited spiritual phrases such as "God is peace," "God is joy," and "God is love." For skeptics uncomfortable with the word "God," researchers allowed substitutions such as "Mother Earth," "the universe," or "my higher self." All participants practiced their method daily over the two weeks preceding the test.[4]

The moment of truth arrived. Each participant began by repeating their practiced technique for twenty minutes, then plunged a hand into the icy bath. As seconds ticked by, researchers recorded every grimace, every twitch.

The results were unmistakable: The spiritual group endured the cold hand plunge nearly twice as long as the others. Participants from all groups rated the pain as equally intense, yet those who meditated on spiritually meaningful phrases seemed to unlock an astonishing hidden reservoir of resilience and endurance. They also reported feeling calmer, less anxious, and generally happier. Even participants who replaced the word "God" with terms of personal significance experienced the powerful benefits.

This study, along with many others, reveals an unexpected truth about prayer: Its power doesn't rest on certainty or dogma. The benefits are accessible even without faith.

This goes back to a distinction we explored in chapter 1:

Fact: An objective truth, verifiable through evidence. (Mount Everest is the highest mountain above sea level on Earth.)

Faith: A conviction without need for objective evidence. (God rewards those who follow His laws.)

Belief: A firmly held opinion, open to revision based on new evidence. (Nearly everything we've discussed so far in this book.)

This difference matters. Many people assume, like I once did, that we must choose between fact and faith. We *believe* we can't have faith in something we don't know as a fact. We become trapped in a false dichotomy: Either accept religious dogma with absolute certainty or abstain entirely.

However, when we engage deeply with ideas we find meaningful, whether we call them God, love, nature, or higher self, we tap into reservoirs of resilience that ordinary thought cannot reach. While such meditation doesn't erase life's inevitable pains, it equips us with internal resources to face difficulties with greater strength. This perspective may offer relief to individuals who yearn for a more pragmatic approach to spiritual practices, one that focuses less on metaphysical correctness and more on experiential results.

But many people find these practices out of reach. A growing number now describe themselves as "spiritual but not religious"—22 percent of Americans and 11 percent of Western Europeans. In the US, this shift has fueled the closure of thousands of churches each year.[5] Many abandoned traditional religious practices, such as prayer, because they couldn't reconcile faith claims with their rational understanding of the world.[6] The result is often the loss of this powerful, psychologically protective practice.

Ironically, research consistently shows that spiritual-but-not-religious people often suffer the most. They report higher rates of anxiety, phobias, and depression, with nearly triple the risk of depression compared to people with no religious identity.[7] These statistics suggest that they may be caught in a philosophical no-man's land, yearning for a transcendent experience but lacking the practices to access it. Of course, prayer can also backfire if it becomes avoidance—asking for rescue instead of taking responsibility, or acting out of fear of divine punishment.[8] However, decades of research show a different pattern overall: Prayer practices generate measurable improvements in well-being, regardless of one's faith.

The way forward isn't to abandon reason or pure skepticism. Prayer and ritual can serve as bridges—acts that help us engage life's mysteries without demanding certainty.

Throughout this chapter, we'll explore how to access these benefits, whatever your starting point. If you practice with faith, science can help you understand and deepen your practice. But even without faith, prayer and ritual still offer profound benefits through universal psychological mechanisms that transcend religious boundaries. Most importantly, you don't need certainty for prayer; you simply need the willingness to engage with practices that humans have found transformative for millennia.

The Purpose of Prayer

Anthropologists note that prayer practices are found in every known human society and predate the development of writing, pottery, farming, and the wheel.[9] When ancient peoples faced unpredictable harvests, inexplicable diseases, or natural disasters, religious ritual offered a way to respond rather than merely endure. By lighting candles, reciting prayers, or performing ceremonies, humans have long recast passive suffering into something actionable.

For years, I misunderstood these ancient practices. I saw prayer as ruminating thoughts spoken to no one, accomplishing nothing. I couldn't have been more wrong. Research by cognitive scientist Eleanor Schille-Hudson reveals that prayer functions as a structured form of thinking. When we pray, we naturally employ a four-step process: articulating the challenge clearly, formulating possible approaches, committing to action, and reflecting on outcomes. Unlike rumination's circular worry, prayer creates what Schille-Hudson calls *collaborative problem-solving*, allowing us to focus on what we can control while delegating the rest to a higher power. Those who pray are left feeling more empowered and optimistic about change.[10]

Growing up in the United States, I'd always thought you were either someone who believed in God, an atheist (someone who didn't), or an agnostic if you weren't sure. But in Singapore, I discovered a new perspective. On a residency form, there was a category I'd never seen before: *free thinker.*

As I came to understand it, a free thinker could be Christian, Muslim, Buddhist, Hindu, Jewish, or none of the above. What distinguishes free thinkers isn't their faith tradition, but how they arrive at their convictions. Free thinkers test ideas against reason, evidence, and experience. They adopt what proves helpful and set aside what doesn't. This small discovery transformed my perspective on my own spiritual journey. Perhaps I didn't need to abandon prayer entirely. Approached as a free thinker, prayer didn't have to involve declarations of certainty or proofs of God's existence. Perhaps prayer and ritual could cultivate what I call the Third Power of Belief: agency.

Singapore made this perspective come alive. Residents find nothing remarkable about the fact that a Catholic church, a Jewish synagogue, a Muslim mosque, a Buddhist temple, and a Hindu mandir can be found on the same street, often side by side. Each religion represents not just a different approach to the divine but potentially a different understanding of what belief itself means.

Living in this rare oasis of religious coexistence, I designed a personal experiment. I would visit each of these traditions and pose the same direct question to their spiritual leaders: "How do I pray to God if I'm not sure He's real?"

My quest wasn't to find the "true" religion or achieve a sudden epiphany. Meeting five leaders could never capture all that their traditions hold. What I wanted to know was simpler: Could these ancient traditions hold wisdom for those of us who dwell in the space between knowing and not-knowing, between fact and faith? What could some of the world's largest religious traditions teach me about prayer and ritual that might transcend their specific theological differences? Could there be ways to engage with those practices meaningfully, even without faith?

Action Before Understanding

Rabbi Mordechai welcomed me through a door located in the kosher grocery store attached to the synagogue. Floor-to-ceiling bookshelves wrapped around the entire room, a testament to centuries of commentary and debate. Ancient leather-bound volumes with faded gold Hebrew lettering stood alongside dog-eared modern paperbacks, their spines cracked from frequent consultation. The air held the musty perfume of old paper and binding glue, as if knowledge itself had a scent. A small wooden desk sat in the center, with just enough space cleared for our conversation.

"Can one pray without certainty about God?" My voice was quieter than I intended.

The gray-bearded Orthodox rabbi didn't respond with theological arguments or scriptural defenses. Instead, he offered something unexpected: permission to question.

"Yeah. Sure," he replied casually, as if I'd asked whether it might rain tomorrow. "We're minute little specks of nothing," he said, studying his hand as if noticing an invisible ant crawling across his thumb. "You pray to a God that is precisely above intellect and transcendent by very definition. So how can anyone be certain about such an unknowable thing?"

Rabbi Mordechai pointed to a fundamental concept in Jewish tradition, drawn from the moment at Mount Sinai when the Israelites declared, "Na'aseh v'nishma": "We will do, and we will hear." Practice first. Understanding follows.

"Everything is about practice," gesturing to the books surrounding us. "A person's psyche is impacted by what he does, not just what he thinks."

He shared how rituals guide us to confront aspects of ourselves that we might otherwise ignore. "How do you change yourself? Some people say therapy—go, sit down on the couch, work it out in the mind." He shook his head. "But you want to change yourself? Start to do."

To illustrate this principle, he described the practice of keeping the Sabbath. More than a religious obligation, the Sabbath creates an "oasis in time." "By disconnecting from the mundane aspects of life once a week—no phones, no work, no rushing—observers [of the Sabbath] begin to experience benefits that transcend simple religious observance."

The rhythm of this practice, he explained, gradually reveals insights about time, rest, and human connection. "Let me tell you," he added with a knowing smile, "many non-Jews I know now observe Shabbat. Maybe they don't do it on Saturday—they do it on Tuesday—but they do it."

Ritual creates regular opportunities to embody our better selves. "It forces you to deal with that particular aspect of your personality, that specific character trait, and to say, 'I've got to counterbalance it.'" Because we rarely notice when we're being selfish, gossipy, or unkind, ritual becomes a practice of embodying the values we aspire to. The doing itself becomes the path to transformation.

Whether weekly or daily, ritual creates a rhythm that changes how people live. Rabbi Mordechai gave a simple example. "It's easy to feel ungrateful. So we start the day with a simple sentence. A Jew starts the day by saying, 'Modeh ani'—'Thank you.' Gratitude. Imagine beginning every single morning with gratitude for being alive."

This was only my first stop on a journey that would reshape my understanding of prayer. Before leaving his office, I asked Rabbi Mordechai if he could connect me with others who could answer the same questions about prayer. The next day, he sent me to the Masjid Ba'alwie, where I met the rabbi's friend, Imam Habib Hassan Alattas.

Submission to Repetition

At the mosque, Hasan, the imam's middle-aged son, ushered me into his father's chambers, a room lined with pictures of dignitaries from neighboring presidents to the UK's King Charles. Imam Alattas entered, his presence warm but commanding. Before I could ask him my questions, he offered me lunch. "You will join us? We ordered kosher food for you." I don't keep kosher, but the thoughtfulness behind the gesture caught me off guard.

As we sat in a dining room for receiving guests, I did my best to follow along. I set aside my fork and ate only with my right hand. After I had licked my fingers clean, we returned to his study, where I posed my question: Can one pray without certainty about God?

The imam seemed puzzled. The only reason someone might doubt, he implied, was because they hadn't had a proper upbringing. "It's all from the parents. Because if your environment, if your parents or your elders guided you, you definitely will know. But if you are not guided from a young age, then you can't see anything."

Since the idea that someone could reach adulthood without certainty about God didn't resonate, I turned to the purpose of prayer in Islam. "Islam is a simple religion. We pray five times a day," he said. "If you can pray on time, good. If unable, you may pray later." Each of the five daily prayers corresponds loosely with natural breaks in the day: morning, midday, late afternoon, evening, and night. "Just like how we eat—breakfast, lunch, tea, dinner, supper," he added.

"It's always the same verses," Imam Alattas added. There's no demand for eloquence, no pressure to invent new words each time. Just return to the same familiar phrases, the same posture, the same rhythm, day after day. A well-known quote from the hadith instructs that in Islam, simplicity is by design. "The religion is easy and no one burdens himself in religion but that it overwhelms him."[11]

But simplicity, in the imam's view, wasn't spiritual minimalism—it was moral reinforcement. "Prayer is to be conscious that God is watching whatever you do," he told me. "If someone makes you angry, prayer is the time to calm down, to leave everything in the hands of God." In a world full of triggers and temptations, he explained, prayer interrupts the momentum of emotion. It's a reset, a re-centering. "You face the world," he said, "and then you pray. It pulls you back. It protects the heart."

I found myself thinking about how rare that kind of structure is in most modern, secular life. We often resist ritual, or we inflate it into something elaborate, like a weeklong retreat or a long ceremony, which makes it difficult to sustain. But here was a case for the opposite: A ritual's power comes from its simplicity and repeatability.

Research confirms this wisdom. Veterans trained to silently repeat a sacred word or phrase of their choosing throughout the day—during stressful moments or while waiting in line—reported significant reductions in stress and improvements in quality of life after just five weeks. No special setting or extended time commitment, just the simple act of returning to a phrase whenever life became overwhelming.[12]

If someone were to design a secular version of prayer, the first principle could be to keep it simple enough to return to again and again. A few short phrases. A familiar gesture. A moment of pause. Perhaps not addressed to a higher power, but still a space to reflect on our values, check our impulses, and remember what kind of person we want to be. We don't forget what's important all at once. We gradually forget over the course of each day. By making prayer short, familiar, and nonnegotiable, Islam builds remembering into the rhythm of forgetting.

Before I left, Imam Alattas handed me a small journal adorned with Islamic art. "For your reflections," he said. I hadn't yet written a word in it, but receiving it felt like a beginning. Maybe I wouldn't pray five times a day, but perhaps I could sit still for a few minutes. Maybe I could repeat one idea I didn't want to forget. And maybe, in a world that rewards novelty, I could learn to respect the quiet strength of doing the same thing, over and over again.

Looking Within

My next stop was with Swami Samachittananda, who welcomed me in traditional monastic robes. His office was sparse, holding just a few photographs, including one of Ramakrishna, the revered nineteenth-century Hindu mystic who taught the unity of all religions.

"Prayer," the swami began, "is for something subjective. Prayer should be for that experience within you."

When I asked about certainty in prayer and belief in the supernatural, the swami gently tapped his chest. "God is not outside somewhere... Within me is what? That is our consciousness, that is the eternal presence of God, and that is the kingdom of heaven."

To illustrate, he shared a personal anecdote. One day at lunch, he casually remarked that the dish needed salt. Immediately, a fellow swami challenged him: "Why do you complain to the cook? There is salt right on your table—just take some." Swami Samachittananda quietly smiled and recalled, "In my mind, that was a problem, but the truth was right there, in front of me. Problems exist only because we think they are problems."

His words reminded me that many of our so-called problems are not facts, but rather perceptions—an idea we discussed earlier in this book. Hindu practice, especially asceticism, further develops this concept by intentionally embracing hardship through fasting, sacrifice, and discomfort. By testing the limits of what we think we cannot live without, we discover how much of our suffering is optional.

Listening to the swami, I began to reflect on what secular prayer might borrow from Hinduism. Prayer doesn't start with asking for external changes. It begins with looking inward, recognizing what is fleeting and what endures. "Anything objective, like money, health, relationships, is transient," the swami explained. In Hinduism, God is not a magic genie that grants wishes. God is consciousness. Every conscious living thing is a reflection of the divine.

So then, what should we pray for? "The only thing to pray for is truth," he said simply. Not truth about how the world might change, but truth about how it already is. Happiness passes. Sadness passes. Wealth and health come and go. What remains is consciousness itself.

The swami's words echoed softly in the quiet room, blending

seamlessly with the serene simplicity around us. I departed, reflecting deeply on his words: Perhaps the real value of prayer, whether secular or spiritual, is not to change life's circumstances but to see them more clearly. To recognize what is passing, to hold fast to what endures, and to live more fully in the present, even learning to love it as it is.

Answering Prayers Through Community

When I first met Father Adrian Danker at the Church of the Sacred Heart, I was struck by his thoroughly unpriestly appearance. Rather than a flowing robe or solemn collar, he wore a simple polo shirt with a school logo: unassuming, approachable, more like a high school teacher or coach than a clergyman.

Our conversation quickly deepened from casual introductions to reflections on prayer. When I asked him about prayer's effectiveness despite doubt, Father Adrian leaned forward with a knowing smile: "Doubt is actually a blessing. It invites reflection, deeper questioning, and ultimately, a richer understanding."

Prayer, he explained, is an ongoing conversation, an act of listening and speaking that helps us find clarity, purpose, and direction. "Prayer invites us to get off our butts," Father Adrian added with a laugh that perfectly matched his high school coach style, "to move from contemplation into action."

He observed that when people pray, they don't merely recite requests. They bring conflicts, anxieties, hopes, and griefs and leave with fresh perspectives, renewed commitments, and sometimes even the courage to reconcile or act where they once felt powerless.

However, the most striking aspect of our conversation was his emphasis on the communal nature of prayer. Every week, parishioners submit petitions: "Lord, help my daughter find a job . . . Please heal my illness . . . Help me find love." These prayers aren't always answered in the ways people expect—or sometimes at all.

"Yet people keep coming," Father Adrian explained, his eyes crinkling at the corners. "Maybe God's answer isn't immediate or obvious, but in returning week after week, they find community. They discover others who listen, support, and offer solutions. Through that communal support, their prayers are often answered in unexpected, tangible ways."

Prayer draws people together, breaking through the epidemic of isolation in modern life. When we gather in communal rituals, whether in churches, temples, or informal settings, we create what sociologists call *collective effervescence,* that electric feeling of connection that emerges when people unite in shared experience.[13]

Research shows that humans are neurobiologically wired for connection. Our nervous systems function more effectively in the presence of supportive others.[14] Our bodies respond to prolonged isolation with increased inflammation, compromised immune function, and heightened stress responses.[15] Ritual spaces offer something increasingly rare: authentic presence with others willing to witness our vulnerabilities, hopes, and existential questions. We don't just enjoy community—we require it.

For secular individuals, this insight proves invaluable. Ritual gatherings, even when detached from supernatural belief, can fulfill our innate need for connection. We need other people to thrive, solve problems, find love, and create a sense of belonging.

"When we pray with expectation," Father Adrian said calmly, "we demand specific results. But praying with hope means trusting something good will come, even if it isn't exactly what we asked for."

That optimistic openness is a universal lesson in adaptability and resilience. As I left, I realized that in his view, the miracle wasn't in God bending to our words. Rather, it was in people coming together, carrying one another's burdens, and answering prayers through human connection.

Transcending Suffering

Singapore's Buddha Tooth Relic Temple was alive with sound and color when I arrived. Monks and devotees chanted in resonant harmony, their voices rising and falling in ancient cadence. The temple stood majestic, its walls painted deep crimson and adorned with intricate carvings that brought Buddhist teachings to life. Golden statues gleamed under carefully placed lighting while wisps of incense perfumed the air, creating an atmosphere of tranquility.

As I moved through the sacred space, I observed worshippers in states of deep reverence—some bowed with practiced precision, while others had their eyes closed in meditation. Away from the main chamber's melodic chanting, I found myself in a modest office where I met Venerable You Guang. I addressed him respectfully as *Shifu*, meaning "teacher." His welcome was genuine, his movements deliberate as he gestured for me to sit. His voice carried a gentle authority; each word seemed carefully weighed before being offered, as though language itself was a sacred gift not to be squandered.

I came with the impression that Buddhism, so often associated with mindfulness in American wellness circles, might offer a more secular-friendly approach to prayer. While Shifu accepted the possibility of practicing without full faith, he emphasized what would be missing.

"Embracing the full narrative of Buddhism provides the necessary context and depth that support a holistic and profound engagement with its teachings." His statement underscored his conviction in the mystical foundation of Buddhism. He spoke of karma and reincarnation, even affirming that suffering, including something as devastating as a child's terminal illness, can be explained by actions in past lives. "You can say it's unfair . . . but in a bigger macro level, there is a certain fairness to things." In that moment, I recognized my inability to embrace a worldview that interpreted children's suffering as cosmic retribution. Yet just as I felt our philosophical divide widening, Shifu sensed my discomfort and pivoted with empathy, suggesting that suffering might serve purposes beyond our immediate understanding. He elaborated that karma, while seemingly harsh, actually empowers individuals through the promise that mindful actions can reshape destinies.

I was surprised to learn that before he had donned the saffron robes of a monk, Shifu was a soldier in Singapore's honor guard for the Istana, the presidential palace. The position required extraordinary physical discipline, including standing motionless in the sweltering heat during five-hour shifts. His coping mechanism was prayer, reciting the Great Compassion mantra. "Even something simple like standing guard duty becomes meaningful when I chant," he explained with quiet conviction. "It keeps my mind grounded and focused, helping me handle long periods of standing and physical discomfort."

Many Buddhists engage in prostrations, full-body bows performed hundreds or even thousands of times in a row. These practices serve as forms of training, transforming suffering into resilience. The lesson has counterparts in other traditions: Muslims fast from dawn to sunset during Ramadan while maintaining their work and family obligations; Jews abstain from all food and water for twenty-five hours during Yom Kippur. By willingly embracing difficulty within a meaningful framework, practitioners discover they can endure far more than they imagined. This revelation expanded my understanding of Buddhist prayer. It does not eliminate suffering. It reframes it—turning hardship into a path of strength.

Universal Patterns

As I stepped back into Singapore's humid heat, I felt an unexpected surge of empowerment. Despite their differences, the practices seemed to be grounded in fundamental aspects of human cognition and experience—universal ways humans use ritual to make sense of uncertainty and find strength.

- **Action before understanding (Jewish):** Ritual practice shapes us even before we fully grasp its meaning.
- **Submission to repetition (Muslim):** Short, familiar rituals reset our emotions and bring us back to what matters.
- **Looking within (Hindu):** The deepest prayer seeks truth and clarity inside, not external change.
- **Answering through community (Christian):** Prayer's power often comes through one another.
- **Transcending suffering (Buddhist):** Ritualized difficulty turns pain into resilience.

None of these tenets is exclusive to just one faith; I heard echoes in every holy space I visited. These principles, taken together, distill complex religious traditions and sometimes-contradictory perspectives into something simpler: the universal mechanisms that give prayer and ritual their strength.

The Wizard of Michigan

If ritual works through human psychology rather than theology, then its power should also be evident outside sacred spaces. In Michigan, one atheist discovered similar principles by creating his own rituals, complete with a wizarding robe.

Garrison Benson managed a movie theater, where he absorbed frequent tirades from customers upset about spilled popcorn, sticky floors, and soda mishaps. The daily barrage left him emotionally drained. So he did what any rational skeptic with an interest in the occult might do: He dressed up as a wizard, went into the woods on his rural property, and cast a magic spell.[16]

Benson placed his movie theater name badge on a tree stump in the silent winter forest. He performed his short ritual by circling the stump nine times. "I imagined the forces of the land, of my home, coming out of the ground, out of the woods, and channeling into the badge, powering it up and creating a sense of emotional safety." With his badge now "enchanted," Benson returned to work. The next time an angry patron yelled at him about their kid's spilled soda, he tapped his badge and pictured their negative energy dissolving into nothing.

The small act of tapping served as a powerful cue. It reminded Benson that "in the moment, this doesn't have anything to do with me personally." Performing this ritual during confrontations helped him sidestep the negative emotions. "If you're able to deal with things in the moment, it can save you a lot of brooding later on. Unresolved, most of us tend to replay those conversations in our heads," he explained. Psychologists would call this "mental distancing," a well-studied psychotherapy practice.

On his podcast *Placebo Magick*, Benson (as his wizard alter-ego Durmak) explains "why and how to cast spells, brew potions, commune with spirits, and hack the human brain, all while understanding that magick isn't real." It's ritual as an honest placebo, deliberately designed to work through the mind rather than the supernatural.

Without realizing it, Benson had stumbled onto the same methods I'd seen across religious traditions. He performed the ritual before fully comprehending how (or if) it worked. He repeated a simple, familiar gesture that reset his emotions. He focused inward, on his own response, rather than requesting a change from his customers. And he used a structured practice to transcend life's discomforts in a stressful environment.

In his book *Ritual: How Seemingly Senseless Acts Make Life Worth Living*, anthropologist Dimitris Xygalatas explains why such practices matter. He explains that rituals provide predictability that "imposes order on the chaos of everyday life, which provides us with a sense of control over uncontrollable situations."[17] Further research confirms that secular rituals can be just as effective as religious ones in reducing anxiety and enhancing performance, provided they incorporate similar structural elements, such as repetition, formality, and symbolic meaning.

Benson's practice may have looked eccentric, but its effects were real. In the woods of Michigan, he rediscovered traditions that had been practiced for centuries and that science now validates. Ritual works because it anchors us in action. It steadies us when we feel powerless, brings order to what seems chaotic, and helps us make sense of our emotions.

The Community Problem

Benson's ritual worked because it provided him with a better way to cope with daily stress. However, rituals have also served another purpose: They bind groups together. This raises a dilemma facing many today: What should someone do when they want the benefits of ritual, prayer, and community, but struggle to find people who share their outlook? How do you connect without pretending to a certainty you don't hold?

The reality is sobering. Attempts to create purely secular alternatives have struggled. The Sunday Assembly, founded in 2013 as an "atheist church," expanded rapidly to seventy chapters worldwide, only to see about half close their doors within a decade.[18] The Ethical Culture movement, despite its 150-year history and humanist ideals, maintains only about twenty active societies in the US.[19] The European Humanist Federation, which comprised over sixty groups, formally dissolved in 2022.[20]

While individual beliefs can be held flexibly for personal benefit, communities require something more binding. If the purpose of my practice is solely personal enhancement, then it's easy to set it aside on the days I don't feel like participating. Without the weight of obligation—often reinforced in religion through the idea of some divine punishment—individual convenience outweighs collective commitment. Religious communities persist not because everyone shares similar beliefs, but because members feel accountable to something greater than themselves.

For me, the answer isn't retreating into isolation or endlessly searching for a flawless secular alternative. It's recognizing that existing religious communities have solved the sustainability problem over centuries of trial and error. Rather than starting from scratch, we might reimagine our relationship with existing institutions and explore better ways of engaging with them. This is where what I call *constructive translation* can be helpful. When the ice-challenge study participants substituted personally meaningful terms, such as "Mother Earth," for "God," they retained the benefits of the practice.

Similarly, when I spoke with the swami and the Buddhist teacher, each revealed that what appeared to be polytheistic pantheons—statues of Shiva, Ganesh, or various fortune deities—actually represent ideas and attributes rather than literal beings. The "gods" are metaphors wrapped in stories pointing to more profound truths.

We can apply this principle to any place of worship. When others speak of God's love, perhaps you hear it as universal compassion. When they reference divine will, you might understand it as the natural order or moral law. When they pray for guidance, you could be seeking wisdom from your highest self. With a bit of mental flexibility, participation becomes possible without dishonesty.

This approach requires a social contract of mutual respect. Religious institutions don't interrogate the precise nature of each member's faith—no one asks whether the Pope wrestles with doubt. In the same spirit, those engaging in constructive translation can respect the literal interpretations of others while holding their own beliefs. The goal isn't to convert anyone but to belong honestly, in your own way. In the end, perhaps the most genuine expression of being a free thinker isn't standing apart from religious community but finding freedom within it—the freedom to interpret, to translate, and to belong without sacrificing intellectual integrity. After all, the human need for community transcends the specific beliefs that set us apart.

Permission to Practice

This chapter began with a six-year-old boy lying on his driveway, talking to God in the pre-dawn darkness. That child didn't question whether God was real—he simply needed someone to talk to, someone who could understand his fears and offer comfort. The practice itself provided solace, regardless of theological certainty.

That is the essence of the Third Power of Belief, agency—the ability to act on our beliefs even when we're uncertain about their ultimate truth. Prayer and ritual exemplify this power by transforming uncertain beliefs into meaningful practices that shape our minds, strengthen our resilience, and connect us to others.

When we pray or engage in ritual, we're not merely thinking about our values or hopes; we're practicing them. This act reinforces neural pathways, emotional habits, and psychological resilience. The *doing* itself becomes transformative, regardless of our certainty about the metaphysical dimensions of the practice.

Inspired by what I'd learned through my exploration of various religious communities and the scientific literature, I began my own simple ritual. Ten minutes each morning: closing my eyes, focusing on my breath, expressing gratitude for being alive, and asking for strength to meet the day's challenges.

The changes were subtle but undeniable: less anxiety at work, more patience at home, sharper awareness of beauty in ordinary moments. Did divine intervention cause these shifts? Neurochemistry?

Expectation? I no longer worry about the answer. The benefits are real, whatever their source.

As a free thinker, I've come to embrace prayer not as submission to religious dogma but as a practical tool for psychological well-being. Simply put, I pray because it makes my life better.

If you count yourself among those who cannot claim the certainty of faith but find the emptiness of pure skepticism equally unsatisfying, I offer this permission: You can pray anyway. You can speak into the silence, lean on rituals that humans have found meaningful for millennia, and draw strength from them without needing perfect certainty. Through ritual, our beliefs become a bridge to tangible benefits we might otherwise never experience.

FROM LIMITING BELIEFS...	TO LIBERATING BELIEFS...
I should avoid ritual because I can't prove the underlying theology.	I can use prayer as structured problem-solving.
I should wait for perfect philosophical alignment before joining any spiritual community.	"Constructive translation" allows me to participate in communities while interpreting language personally.
My willpower alone should be enough to solve my problems.	Ritual and community support often answer prayers through human connection.
Creating overly complex spiritual practices can't be sustained.	I can start with simple, repeatable rituals.
Prayer is for asking for things to change.	Prayer is for asking for the strength, clarity, and wisdom to overcome challenges.
Spiritual practices should be judged by whether they align with my intellectual beliefs.	I can measure spiritual practices by how they affect my well-being and relationships.

CHAPTER 10

Your Labels Are Your Limits

Beware the beliefs that steal your power.

A TWENTY-SIX-YEAR-OLD MAN BURST into an emergency room gasping for breath and begging for help. "I took all my pills," he exclaimed to the startled staff before collapsing to the floor. As the nurses would later learn, this man, identified in a stunning case study as "Mr. A," was taking part in a clinical drug trial for a new antidepressant and had received a bottle of the medication the day before. Following an upsetting argument with his girlfriend, he'd succumbed to impulse and swallowed all twenty-nine remaining capsules at once. Panicked, he'd asked his neighbor to rush him to the hospital.

Like many other drug overdose victims, Mr. A was gravely ill. His blood pressure had fallen to a dangerously low 80/40. His heart raced—110 beats per minute. His skin was pale and covered in cold sweat. His body trembled uncontrollably as he drifted in and out of consciousness. Doctors rushed to stabilize Mr. A, administering nearly six liters of intravenous fluids over an hour to combat his low blood pressure.

Meanwhile, they tried to figure out what he'd taken. Without this crucial information, they were flying blind, forced to rely on supportive measures while Mr. A's condition worsened. Blood tests showed no trace of common toxins. Fortunately, a physician from the clinical trial arrived to help and revealed the unexpected truth: Mr. A had been randomly assigned to the placebo group in the double-blind study. Every capsule he had consumed was inert. Nothing in the pills could have caused the symptoms he was experiencing.[1]

When the doctors shared this revelation with Mr. A, relief washed over his face. Within fifteen minutes, his condition resolved. His mental fog cleared. His blood pressure normalized. His heart rate settled to eighty beats per minute. This man, who had been deathly ill moments earlier, was suddenly, inexplicably, fine.

Mr. A had experienced severe medical symptoms not from any poison but from his *conviction* that he had overdosed. His brain had accepted this belief as reality, triggering powerful physiological responses that overwhelmed his body. The moment his belief changed, these responses dissipated. His collapse and subsequent recovery each stemmed from the same powerful source: belief.

Trapped by Our Beliefs

There's a scientific term for what Mr. A experienced: the *nocebo* effect. While placebos harness positive expectations to heal, nocebos weaponize *negative* expectations to create suffering.[2] Tell patients that a harmless pill might cause nausea, and many will feel queasy.[3] Warn them about pain, and they'll experience more intense discomfort, even without a physical cause.[4] Inform them that they've been exposed to an allergen, and they'll start sneezing and feeling stuffy.[5]

Nocebo reactions can manifest as almost any symptom, including headaches, rashes, fatigue, dizziness, and chest pain.[6] The underlying cause is anticipation of harm, even when none exists.[7]

Shockingly, nocebo symptoms aren't purely psychological. In fact, they create measurable physiological changes. Just as hope and positive expectations release neurotransmitters like endorphins and dopamine that soothe pain, negative emotions, such as fear and hopelessness, can unleash a bodily response that can weaken immunity and strain the heart.[8] Simply believing that you've ingested a toxin can activate stress responses that release cortisol and histamine, leading to inflammation and heightened pain perception.[9]

In one study, patients receiving a harmless saline solution began vomiting and even lost hair, believing they'd undergone toxic chemotherapy.[10] Their bodies, anticipating that poison was coming, released stress hormones and inflammatory molecules that produced authentic chemotherapy-like side effects.

Nocebo effects aren't confined to medicine. Negative beliefs can distort ordinary experiences. In one study, psychologists Robert Kleck and Angelo Strenta applied fake scars to participants' faces and then allowed them to examine themselves in a mirror.[11] During a supposed touch-up, researchers secretly removed the scars but told participants that the scars remained. When they entered conversations convinced they were disfigured, the participants later reported that their conversation partners seemed uncomfortable, avoided eye contact, and appeared to stare at their (nonexistent) scars.

Participants' belief in their scars created a reality filter that transformed neutral interactions into ordeals of perceived rejection and alienation. Though nothing about their appearance had changed, their sense of social agency diminished. Although they might have wished to feel popular, liked, and accepted, their belief left them feeling alienated and unable to connect with others. They described vivid experiences of discrimination and discomfort, all reactions to a scar that wasn't there.

We often fall into similar negative belief traps ourselves, shaping how we perceive and interact with the world. We erect mental barriers for ourselves that limit what we think we can accomplish, thereby influencing what we *actually* achieve. Think of the labels we give ourselves: "I'm not a morning person," "I'm bad with names," "I just can't focus." Accepting these beliefs, we ignore our morning alarm when it goes off, minimize our efforts to learn others' names, or stop seeking better ways to manage our attention. Over time, those self-imposed limits harden into reality; we really do become more sluggish in the morning or worse at learning names. Without realizing it, we imprison ourselves by surrendering to a single, underlying belief: "I'm not capable."

Negative Beliefs Are Contagious

We may think these limiting beliefs stop with us, but they don't. They move outward, sweeping through groups and communities like wildfire. When others show signs of distress, especially people with whom we identify, our brains often mirror those signals with similar physiological responses. We anticipate that what's happening to others could happen to us, and our bodies react accordingly.

Consider what happened in Portugal in 2006, when hundreds of students across the country suddenly fell ill. They broke out with the same pattern of physical symptoms: rashes, dizziness, and breathing difficulties. Medical authorities thoroughly investigated every possible biological cause, from allergic reactions to chemical exposure and viruses, but found no conclusive evidence. Then came a clue: A popular teen soap opera called *Strawberries with Sugar* had recently aired an episode featuring a fictional life-threatening disease afflicting students. The Portuguese teenagers weren't sick; they were experiencing a nocebo effect on a mass scale. Their expectation of sickness created the physical symptoms they feared.[12]

What happened in Portugal wasn't unique. Similar outbreaks have been reported worldwide. In 1965, eighty-five schoolgirls in Blackburn, England, collapsed in a fainting epidemic.[13] In the 1990s and early 2000s, men in West Africa reported symptoms of koro syndrome, a terrifying belief that their penises were retracting into their bodies.[14] In 2016, more than eighty students in a school in Peru experienced fainting, seizures, and hallucinations.[15] Across these cases, doctors found no toxin, pathogen, or physical explanation. The symptoms arose from belief itself.

These days, social media has taken belief contagion to a new level. Algorithms can spread convincing descriptions of psychological symptoms and mental health diagnoses to millions within seconds, creating digital nocebo effects on an unprecedented scale. Content designed to go viral can spur self-diagnosis in viewers, who adopt not just labels but entire symptom patterns.[16]

The same amplification happens with drug scares. Perhaps you've seen the dramatic police body-camera footage of officers collapsing after coming into contact with fentanyl, a potent synthetic opioid. In a widely circulated video from 2022, a Kansas City cop lies unconscious as colleagues panic, administer doses of Narcan, and rush him to the hospital. Later, the officer recalled, "I knew I was dying."[17] Except he wasn't, nor was he experiencing any overdose. Scientists have shown that brief skin contact with fentanyl can't possibly cause such reactions. Still, after the video spread, more people reported similar reactions. What spread wasn't a chemical, but a conviction.

The Identity Trap

One of the most common ways we unknowingly limit our own agency is by rigidly adopting diagnostic identities. Proper diagnoses serve crucial purposes—guiding effective treatment and helping us understand our challenges more clearly. However, uncritically accepted diagnoses or self-diagnoses can introduce limiting beliefs that reshape not only how we view our circumstances but also how we define our very capabilities. Labels like *burnout*, *ADHD*, and *trauma response* can function as powerful nocebos. The danger lies not in the labels themselves, but in allowing them to become the primary lens through which we interpret our experiences and potential.

Take my friend Thomas (not his real name). By his mid-thirties, he had built a successful career at a demanding tech company. Intelligent, sociable, and deeply curious, he decided to take time off after several particularly stressful quarters to, in his words, "get my head right." His employer supported the break and even covered sessions with a mental health specialist. Within weeks, Thomas received several diagnoses, including generalized anxiety disorder.

When we met for coffee shortly after his diagnosis, Thomas seemed visibly lighter. "It finally makes sense," he said, stirring his latte with unusual animation. "All those times I'd lie awake worrying about presentations or feel like my heart was going to explode before meetings, it wasn't just me being weak. It's this thing I have, this anxiety disorder." He compared the diagnosis to finally seeing the villain in a horror movie after only catching glimpses of its shadow. "Now I know what I'm fighting," he said with genuine relief.

Thomas's initial reaction made sense. A diagnosis can provide structure to what once felt like chaos, offering validation and potential strategies for coping. Having that missing puzzle piece helps people better understand themselves and their challenges. But over the following months, I watched a concerning transformation. Our conversations, once alive and ranging across countless topics from books to professional projects, narrowed to his diagnoses, symptoms, medications, and therapy sessions. He even started backing out of social events, citing his anxiety.

Over a period of years, the diagnosis that initially empowered him became his identity. Rather than seeing himself as a capable person managing anxiety, he began viewing himself as a fundamentally anxious individual. That shift intensified his symptoms and diminished his sense of agency. As author Richard Bach once wrote, "Argue for your limitations, and sure enough they're yours."[18]

How a Diagnosis Becomes Destiny

Thomas's story isn't unusual. Mental health care often unintentionally encourages people to overidentify with their diagnoses. To be clear, diagnostic labels aren't useless; they can validate suffering and provide language for seeking help. But they come with risks. A label can blur the line between a temporary condition and a permanent identity. Psychologists refer to this as *identity foreclosure*, which involves prematurely committing to an identity before adequately exploring alternatives, thereby surrendering agency and closing off other possible identities.[19]

A student who sees themselves as "not a math person" early on, for instance, might avoid the subject altogether, closing doors before they've even tested their limits. Perhaps their dislike stemmed from a poorly taught class that didn't fully develop their aptitude for the subject. But by then, their self-perception prevents them from exploring alternative learning methods.

The same dynamic plays out with medical diagnoses. Someone told they have depression may stop seeing themselves as a person experiencing symptoms and instead as a *depressed person*. As a result, they stop taking action to feel better, reasoning that it's pointless. Over time, their restricted experiences reinforce the identity, turning a diagnosis once meant to guide healing into a self-fulfilling prophecy.

Scholars have documented this process as a form of identity foreclosure. In a 2024 study, Harvard researcher Nick Haslam and colleagues found that labeling someone with generalized anxiety disorder or major depression made both the individual and those around them more pessimistic about their recovery.[20] By contrast, describing the same condition in terms of symptoms ("feels anxious," "has trouble concentrating") produced more hopeful expectations. The label itself diminished not only outsiders' expectations but also the person's own ability to change.

Similarly, children with ADHD frequently internalize their diagnosis into their self-concept.[21] For example, a student who adopts the belief, "I have ADHD, so I can't focus well," is more likely to exert less effort and disengage more quickly, thereby reinforcing their own negative expectations.[22] Likewise, adults newly diagnosed with anxiety disorders may begin to interpret ordinary nervousness as pathological. Thoughts such as, "There goes my anxiety again. I'm going to spiral!" can heighten feelings of helplessness and reduce perceived agency.[23] In both cases, the diagnosis doesn't create the condition, but it can create a narrative that limits what people believe they can handle.

The very language doctors use to describe conditions plays a decisive role. Consider back pain. Tell a patient they have degenerative disc disease, and many will picture their spines disintegrating, prompting them to avoid activity that might help. Call the very same condition "age-related changes," on the other hand, and patients are much more inclined to get out there and move.[24] The words themselves shape patients' understanding of what's happening in their bodies, influencing their behavior, outcomes, and sense of control over their condition.

What begins as a diagnosis can grow stronger when echoed back by others. Support groups and online forums can provide validation and belonging, but they can also encourage overidentification with medical diagnoses and limit the exploration of alternative identities.[25] When conversations revolve exclusively around diagnoses, participants may come to see their condition as the core of who they are. The message "your pain is real, you're not alone" is invaluable. Yet without sufficient recovery narratives, such communities risk sending the message that individuals will always be defined by their trauma or illness.[26]

This overidentification is amplified by a broader cultural shift in how we define illness. Haslam refers to this as "concept creep": the gradual expansion of diagnostic categories.[27] What our grandparents once called "nerves" might now be labeled an anxiety disorder; ordinary sadness may be pathologized as clinical depression. While increased awareness and reduced stigma help many people access needed support, they also pathologize everyday human struggles, reducing our sense of agency over ordinary emotional responses.

Professor Francesca Happé of King's College London observes that most Britons now consider themselves neurodivergent, identifying with common mental health conditions. "Once you take autism, ADHD, dyslexia, dyspraxia and all the other ways that you can developmentally be different from the typical, you actually don't get many typical people left."[28] Duke University psychiatrist Allen Frances quips, "Modern medicine is making such rapid advances, soon none of us will be well."[29]

None of this means we should discard diagnoses. For many, they relieve suffering and provide language for real struggle. For others, they can become limiting identities that restrict agency and hope. The test is functional: Does this label help you take effective action, seek support, and grow, or does it sap your initiative and shrink your sense of self?

That is why addiction researchers avoid calling people "addicts." They know that labels stick. A person described as "an addict" is cast as broken. Instead, a person described as "struggling with impulse control" is separated from the diagnosis; it becomes something they face, not something they are. Similarly, thinking of yourself as someone who "currently finds it difficult to concentrate" rather than "I have ADHD" frames your current struggle as something you can overcome rather than a permanent identity. It paints a picture of someone in motion, someone with choices, someone who can change. The difference is more than semantics; it's living under constraint versus acting with power.

When used correctly, labels resemble a map that helps you chart the way through the challenges ahead. The danger comes when we overidentify with illnesses, allowing the diagnosis to become our destiny.

When "Safety" Hurts

Just as diagnoses can unintentionally narrow our sense of possibility, so too can certain therapeutic practices. To avoid retraumatizing vulnerable people, for example, some therapists advocate strategies like trigger warnings, safe spaces, and constant validation. And yet, like medical language and diagnoses, these well-intentioned measures can inadvertently send a message that people lack the power to handle life's difficulties.

In a university setting, a professor might issue a trigger warning to students before discussing potentially upsetting material, giving trauma survivors the option to prepare or opt out. However, research suggests that these warnings rarely reduce distress; in some cases, they actually *heighten* anxiety by reinforcing a sense of vulnerability.[30] Well-intentioned as they are, trigger warnings can function as psychological nocebos, priming people to feel more fragile than they actually are.

In the clinic, a therapist who encourages clients to avoid uncomfortable situations may inadvertently lower their tolerance for pain. While the client feels temporarily safer, their world becomes increasingly constrained. Each act of avoidance tells the brain, "That was unmanageable. We were right to escape."

As we saw in chapter 8, helplessness is not something we learn; rather, it is our default state. Agency, the belief that our actions count, must be built. Trigger warnings, safe spaces, and overprotection, however well-meant, train the opposite of resilience and self-reliance.

For many patients, anxiety about being retraumatized leads to avoidance. Avoidance provides short-term relief, and relief teaches the brain that avoidance is the only safe option. The result: Anxiety grows more debilitating at every subsequent encounter. Breaking this cycle requires gently *challenging* fears that expand the individual's world. Agency grows not from avoiding discomfort, but from proving, again and again, that we can survive it.

Flawed Memories Can Become Limiting Beliefs

Trauma-focused therapy starts with a reasonable premise: that difficult experiences shape us. But when the focus leans too heavily on excavation, patients risk becoming trapped in a damage-centered lens. The unspoken message becomes: *Your pain defines you.* Without equal emphasis on strengths and skills, therapy can reinforce helplessness rather than restore agency.

Validating suffering matters, but so does helping people see themselves as more than their past. Research indicates that the way trauma is integrated into one's identity plays a significant role in recovery outcomes.[31] Individuals who make their trauma central to their identity often experience worse long-term outcomes than those who acknowledge trauma without making it the core of their self-concept.[32]

The problem grows more complex when we rely on recollections. We navigate life believing that our memories accurately record our past, but research shows that remembering functions as a reconstruction, not a recording. Every act of recall subtly rewrites memories by layering in current emotions, beliefs, emotional needs, and external inputs. While this doesn't mean traumatic events didn't happen, it does suggest our relationship to them is less fixed than we think. At the extreme, we are capable of carrying entire self-narratives based on events that never occurred.

Consider the case of Chris. For decades, he believed he couldn't cry because of a traumatic childhood experience: attending the funeral of a beloved cousin who had committed suicide. Since that day, Chris says, he remained stoic, unable to shed tears even in moments of deep emotion. Years later, however, a conversation with his sister and mother revealed that he had never actually attended the funeral. His inability to cry wasn't tied to trauma at all but to a *false belief* that had become self-reinforcing.[33]

Memory researcher Dr. Elizabeth Loftus has demonstrated how easily false memories can take root. In her famous "lost in the mall" study, roughly 25 percent of participants came to believe, and vividly recall, being lost in a shopping mall, even though no such event ever happened.[34] This study, along with others like it, reveals the malleability of human memory and how convincingly false recollections can be woven into one's identity.[35]

This malleability carries profound implications for trauma-focused therapy. In the 1980s and 1990s, countless patients underwent therapy that supposedly "recovered" repressed memories of childhood abuse. Many of these memories were later proven to be false, having been implanted by suggestion. The consequences were devastating: Lives were ruined, families torn apart, and innocent people imprisoned.[36] To this day, some therapists encourage clients to search for repressed memories, a concept popularized by Sigmund Freud, despite the scientific consensus that there is "no credible scientific evidence that repressed memories exist."[37]

All of this raises an uncomfortable but essential question: Are the stories we tell about our past serving us, or keeping us stuck? Some memories of past hardships provide valuable wisdom and self-protection. Others become tales we repeat, reinforcing helplessness rather than growth.

True healing comes not from endlessly excavating the past but from loosening our grip on those stories enough to create room for new ones. By reframing the stories we tell about our past and the meanings behind them, we open space to act in the present.

Pills Don't Teach Skills

Just as trauma-focused therapy risks reinforcing helplessness, so can an overreliance on medication. In the United States, medication is still widely seen as the first-line response for common psychological distress, especially for children and young adults whose brains are still developing. Prescriptions promise quick fixes, but the expectation of rapid relief from a pill alone can prevent the development of resilience, leaving people less prepared to handle life's difficulties and more dependent on external solutions.

Gordon Marino, a philosophy professor at St. Olaf College, describes how his Ritalin prescription initially helped him focus but rapidly became a dependency that left him feeling disempowered. "Instead of helping to maintain my self-confidence during a veritable earthquake in my life," Marino writes, "my need for a crutch in pill form radically undermined my faith in myself."[38] Marino's experience isn't unique: Medications can provide symptom relief, but they operate at the biochemical level, rather than the behavioral one. Even when they work precisely as intended, they don't teach us the skills we need, like cognitive frameworks, emotional regulation techniques, and practical habits, to develop a genuine sense of agency.

Skill-building therapies, such as cognitive behavioral therapy, do far more than just reduce symptoms. They give ownership back to the individual. Skills are transferable: What helps with anxiety might also alleviate procrastination or resolve conflicts at work. Skills become practices that endure long after the effects of the pill wear off. They also nurture a high-agency mindset, encouraging people to view challenges as opportunities for growth rather than permanent limitations that require chemical solutions.

For some patients, medication remains a critical treatment tool and can be lifesaving, especially for those suffering from severe depression, bipolar disorder, and schizophrenia. Yet even in these cases, the best outcomes typically result from combining pharmacological approaches with therapy, skills training, and life changes that foster agency.

Skill development indeed requires more effort than taking a pill, because it asks us to face uncomfortable emotions rather than numb them. But this productive struggle becomes the pathway to growth. The saying often attributed to Viktor Frankl captures this idea: "Between stimulus and response, there is a space. In that space lies our power to choose our response."[39]

Research across mental health diagnoses affirms that skill-building therapies often produce better long-term outcomes than medication. In depression, medication may work faster initially, but therapy wins the race in the long run.[40] Studies of anxiety and ADHD show the same pattern.[41] Pills may provide temporary relief, but they don't teach the skills needed to thrive amid life's challenges.

Reclaiming Our Agency

If therapy and medication risk narrowing our sense of possibility, the way forward is to reclaim ownership of the beliefs and labels we live by. Diagnoses and prescriptions can be essential, but a prognosis represents, at best, an educated guess. It is only a starting point for the healing process, not a verdict on our potential.

Writer Matt Haig, who has lived with depression, ADHD, and autism, warns against turning labels into identities: "It can be dangerous to set ourselves in stone."[42] He cautions against thinking, "I am like this because I have x or y or z, so I will keep acting like this because that is who I am." Haig offers a way forward: "Sometimes you need to say, 'No, I can be better.' And by embracing that possibility, we can change."

Recall Mr. A's overdose incident: His body collapsed not because of toxicity but because of belief. Once his belief changed, his body followed. We can do the same by examining the stories and labels we adopt and asking, "Does this belief expand or contract my capacity to act effectively?"

Every day, we are handed beliefs about what we can and cannot do. If we accept those beliefs uncritically, they can become traps. However, through careful assessment of our beliefs, we can reject those that don't serve us and embrace those that give us the strength to move forward. When we choose our labels carefully, we don't just change how we see the world—we change what becomes possible within it.

FROM LIMITING BELIEFS...	TO LIBERATING BELIEFS...
My diagnosis defines who I am and what I'm capable of.	My diagnosis is information based on my experiences, not my identity.
If someone tells me that I can't change, I should accept it.	Prognoses are educated guesses, not verdicts.
I need to avoid anything that might trigger or upset me.	I can handle discomfort and grow stronger by facing challenges gradually.
My painful memories are fixed truths that control my present.	My relationship with the past is flexible. I can reframe stories that no longer serve me.
Taking medication means I'm broken and need fixing.	I can use tools like medication while building my own skills and capabilities.
I should focus on understanding why I'm damaged.	I can acknowledge my struggles while building on my strengths and capitalizing on my potential.

Important Note

You've seen how agency transforms belief into action and how small wins build lasting confidence. To help you carry that momentum forward, I've created bonus resources that will strengthen your sense of agency and open the door to new growth. You'll also discover ongoing research and fresh strategies to support you beyond these pages.

Go to NirAndFar.com/belief-tools/
or scan the QR code below.

CONCLUSION

CHAPTER 11

Good Beliefs, Bad Beliefs

Why your dreams might be sabotaging your goals—and what to do instead.

THE MOLES APPEARED without warning—small, angry red bumps that looked like clusters of blood vessels pushing through David's skin. For weeks, David asked every doctor and nurse who stepped into his hospital room the same desperate question: "What do these moles mean?"

Everyone dismissed him. David's liver was failing, his kidneys were shutting down, and his bone marrow had stopped producing blood cells. Why fixate on harmless skin blemishes? But David couldn't let it go. Something told him these seemingly insignificant marks mattered.

At twenty-five, David Fajgenbaum was the picture of American success: a former Division I quarterback at Georgetown, now a medical student at the University of Pennsylvania on full scholarship, and dating his college sweetheart. Then, in July 2010, during what should have been a routine summer break between medical school rotations, Fajgenbaum's carefully constructed world began to collapse.

"Over the course of just a couple of weeks," he later recalled, "I went from being totally healthy... literally winning bench press contests because I was in such good shape, to feeling more tired than I'd ever felt before."[1] Within days, he was blind in one eye from a retinal hemorrhage, swollen with seventy pounds of excess fluid, and reliant on daily blood transfusions just to stay alive.

After eleven excruciating weeks of intensive testing at one of America's premier medical institutions, a diagnosis finally came: HHV-8-negative, idiopathic multicentric Castleman disease. The nurse who delivered the news admitted, almost cheerfully, that she'd never heard of the disease, but assured him at least it wasn't lymphoma.

Alone in his hospital room, Fajgenbaum immediately turned to Google. Whatever comfort the nurse's upbeat delivery had provided was instantly shattered. A 1996 study found that patients with the ultra-rare immune system disorder lived, on average, just one year after diagnosis, and only one in eight lived beyond two. Fajgenbaum broke down in tears.

That could have been the end of his story—but it wasn't.

David Fajgenbaum's survival, and what followed, reveals something profound about the way beliefs shape our lives. Richter's swimming rats showed that belief could turn minutes into hours in the water. Fajgenbaum's belief gave him the same endurance, carrying him through impossible odds. Surrender was never the only option.

He was not superhuman, nor did Fajgenbaum have any mystical gift. What separated him from despair was how he used belief: directing attention to overlooked signals, anticipating possibilities, and taking disciplined action.

This is the story of how limiting beliefs nearly cost Fajgenbaum his life, and how liberating beliefs, expressed through the powers of attention, anticipation, and agency, helped transform him from a dying patient into the architect of his own cure. For Fajgenbaum, helpful beliefs meant the difference between life and death not only for himself but also for countless others.

Beliefs didn't heal Fajgenbaum; they directed him toward the right questions and the next step forward. But beliefs come with a warning: They can either propel us toward action or, when left untethered from effort and evidence, trap us in passivity.

The Negative Side of Positive Thinking

Today, millions of adults worldwide embrace beliefs that promise control over life's uncertainties through mental power alone. Marketed under names like "positive thinking" and "manifesting," these ideas sound helpful and are spread with the best of intentions. Yet, as we'll see, they can often do more harm than good.

Promoted through social media and self-help gurus, positive-thinking approaches instruct us to "vibrate at the frequency of abundance" or to manifest our desires through thought alone. The promises have grown increasingly bold. Self-appointed gurus like Joe Dispenza claim that we can reshape physical reality through visualization. In one of his popular lectures, he explains, "The more coherent my heart is, the more energy in my heart, the more I can draw my future to me."[2] According to this view, you simply need to achieve the right brain state and to "fall in love with that future" to draw it to you, "with the magnetic field of the heart."

Backed by quantum physics buzzwords and misused neuroscience, the sales pitch is seductive: Align your thoughts with your desires, maintain unwavering faith, and watch the universe deliver precisely what you ordered.

This infatuation with positive thinking isn't new. In America, it dates back to the 1800s and Phineas Quimby's "mind cure" movement, which rose in rebellion against the fatalist religious doctrines of the time.[3] By the mid-twentieth century, Norman Vincent Peale, the era's high priest of positive thinking, instructed readers to "stamp indelibly on your mind a mental picture of yourself succeeding" in his bestseller *The Power of Positive Thinking*.[4] Rhonda Byrne updated positive thinking for the twenty-first century with her 2006 book *The Secret*, promising that thoughts alone can bring anything into one's life, including wealth, health, and love.[5] According to Byrne, the law of attraction is as reliable as the law of gravity.

Behind the seductive promises lies an uncomfortable truth: Scientific research shows that positive thinking alone often fails to produce lasting benefits and may even backfire.[6] As journalist Barbara Ehrenreich noted in *Bright-Sided*, her analysis of the positive-thinking industry, the ethos of "positive vibes only" can exact "a terrible price in self-blame" when illness or hardship doesn't simply yield to optimism.[7]

Eventually, reality delivers the truth with a blunt headline: "Wishing Isn't Doing." When positive thinking becomes a substitute for effort, it can prevent us from taking the necessary steps.

When Visualizing Backfires

New York University social psychologist Gabriele Oettingen has demonstrated through decades of research that positive fantasies can actually reduce motivation if we indulge in them in the wrong way.[8] When we imagine the rewards of success without considering the effort required to achieve them, we can "fool our minds into thinking that we've already achieved our goals." That relaxes us and drains the energy we need to take action.

In one particularly revealing experiment, Oettingen demonstrated how fantasy saps our energy on a measurable, physiological level.[9] She and her colleagues hooked participants up to monitors and asked them to visualize their futures. Some participants were asked to imagine vivid, positive outcomes of their most cherished hopes, such as landing a dream job, finding perfect romance, or attaining ideal fitness. Others were instructed to focus on more neutral or realistic possibilities of these same goals. Within minutes, those who adopted positive beliefs experienced a significant drop in their blood pressure. Their bodies behaved as if the goal had already been reached, with their minds signaling, "Mission accomplished. No need to struggle or strive."

From academic tests to weight loss to career advancement, mentally rehearsing victory consistently led to fewer victories in real life. "The more positively people fantasize or dream about their success," Oettingen explains, "the less well they do."

Positive fantasies feel great in the moment. They give us an initial rush of optimism and temporary relief from uncertainty. But like any high, the effect wears off. Unsurprisingly, after the high comes the crash, often accompanied by deeper discouragement when reality fails to match our fantasized expectations.

As members of Oettingen's team dug into their research data, they found a darker side: Positive fantasies could also worsen people's moods. For people struggling with depression, for instance, positive fantasies actually correlated with a higher likelihood of future depressive symptoms. The result is a self-reinforcing cycle I call the Circle of False Promise.

It begins with an uplifting fantasy of achieving our goals. We soon discover that the actual path forward requires far more effort than our dreamland scenarios suggested. The stark disconnect between fantasy and reality often disappoints us, leading us to scale back our efforts or abandon our goal entirely. We come away feeling more helpless and inadequate than we started. The worse our lives feel, the more we try to escape by sinking back into our fantasies about the future. The whole process repeats itself, again and again. Each unfulfilled fantasy becomes further evidence of personal failure. Each unsuccessful attempt at "manifesting" reinforces the belief in our helplessness.

THE CIRCLE OF FALSE PROMISE

Positive fantasy → Brief emotional lift → Reduced motivation → Minimal action → Poor outcomes → Disappointment → Worsening mood → Need for escape → (Positive fantasy)

When fantasy stands in for effort, disappointment feeds helplessness, and the loop repeats.

It's hardly surprising that the positive-thinking industry has an answer for this inconvenient truth. When magical thinking doesn't work, the problem is never with the method; it's always with you. You weren't aligned with your desires. You have resistance that needs clearing. Your vibration wasn't high enough.

This creates a particularly cruel psychological trap. The more you struggle, the more you're told you need to work on yourself. The more it doesn't work, the more you're convinced you're doing it wrong. Meanwhile, you're not developing actual skills, gaining experience, or taking effective action toward your goals. You become stuck in an endless cycle of self-improvement that feels like progress but produces none.

This pattern can be observed beyond New Age manifesting, where certain religious practices ensnare people in similar traps. The well-meaning platitude "let go and let God" can become another form of spiritual bypassing—a way to avoid the difficult work of taking responsibility for what we can control. This doesn't diminish the genuine power of prayer, which we explored in chapter 9. It simply marks the difference between spiritual practices that build agency and those that erode it. Waiting for divine intervention while avoiding effort is just another way of surrendering control. Effective belief systems should inspire action, not replace it. As the saying goes, "God helps those who help themselves."[10]

Unfortunately, our culture has made it increasingly difficult to distinguish between evidence-based belief practices and ineffective look-alikes. The same terminology—belief, visualization, positive thinking, mindset—gets applied indiscriminately to both rigorous scientific applications and dubious pseudoscientific schemes. The same techniques—meditation, prayer, affirmations, goal-setting—appear in both peer-reviewed therapeutic programs and manipulative marketing campaigns. This blurred line between legitimate psychology and snake oil creates confusion for anyone trying to separate what actually works from what merely sounds appealing. The result is a marketplace where science-backed interventions compete for attention with feel-good platitudes that promise miraculous results without substance.

The magical thinking industry deliberately exploits this vulnerability. For example, a manifestation course might start by explaining how visualization activates the same brain regions as actual experience, a genuine finding from neuroscience studies. It might then discuss how athletes use mental rehearsal to improve performance, another legitimate application. However, it then makes an unwarranted leap, claiming that these mechanisms prove we can "attract" external circumstances through thought alone.

The progression seems logical on the surface, but it represents a fundamental misunderstanding of what the research actually shows. For athletes, visualization doesn't make basketball hoops more welcoming or defenders easier to beat. The technique helps because it prepares their brains and bodies for actions they will actually perform. Similarly, the placebo effect demonstrates that expectations can significantly influence our perception of symptoms and side effects. But this doesn't mean we can cure cancer through positive thinking or heal a broken bone with affirmations. The mechanisms are specific, limited, and thoroughly biological, not magical.

Fortunately, we can protect ourselves from these false promises while still reaping the genuine benefits of belief. Visualization works when it primes us for action. Placebos work when paired with appropriate treatment. Positive expectations matter when they lead us to prepare, not when they substitute for effort.

The Santa Claus Theory

When David Fajgenbaum first became ill, he assumed that, somewhere, a team of brilliant scientists was working around the clock to cure his disease. Fajgenbaum called it the "Santa Claus theory"—the comforting belief that answers already exist, and someone else will deliver them.[11] But this assumption came at a steep cost. "Believing that nearly all medical questions are already answered means that all you need to do is find a doctor who knows the answers," Fajgenbaum writes. "And as long as Santa-doctors are working diligently on those diseases for which there are not yet answers, there is no incentive for us to try to push forward progress for these diseases when they affect us or our loved ones."

Fajgenbaum's assumption turned the Three Powers of Belief against him. Through the power of attention, the Santa Claus theory directed Fajgenbaum's focus toward finding the right expert, rather than developing his own understanding of his condition. Through anticipation, it created expectations of external rescue, rather than discovery from within. And through agency, it encouraged passivity, disguised as appropriate deference to authority.

This reflex to outsource shows up everywhere. We wait for politicians to solve complex social problems rather than engaging in local community action. We expect teachers to educate our children with little parental involvement. We assume economists will handle healthcare reform or poverty while we sit on the sidelines.

The turning point for Fajgenbaum came during his fourth near-death episode, when he was hospitalized under the care of Dr. Frits van Rhee, the world's leading expert on Castleman disease. Fajgenbaum had pinned all his hopes on an experimental drug called siltuximab, designed to block the immune system protein thought to be driving his disease. This was his Santa Claus moment, complete with the perfect expert and the perfect treatment that would finally provide the rescue he'd been waiting for.

But that rescue never came. Siltuximab failed. Despite receiving the "miracle drug" that had helped other patients, Fajgenbaum's organs continued shutting down, and his symptoms worsened. Devastated, Fajgenbaum turned to Dr. van Rhee for answers. Surely he'd have a plan for what to do next.

"What causes this to happen?" Fajgenbaum asked.

"No one knows," van Rhee replied.

"Which type of immune cell is responsible for initiating this?"

"No one knows."

"Are there any other drugs in development or clinical trials?"

"No, not at the moment."

"Are there any planned?"

"Not that I'm aware of."

From this brief conversation, Fajgenbaum realized that his fundamental beliefs about the role he'd play in his treatment had to change. Santa Claus wasn't coming.

"The foremost expert in the world can only ever know as much as the accumulated knowledge in the world," Fajgenbaum realized. "If the answers have not yet been uncovered, then the foremost expert couldn't possibly know them." The conversation was both crushing and liberating. "A proper patient might have taken Dr. van Rhee's pronouncements with humility and acceptance," Fajgenbaum writes, "but *no one knows* didn't cut it for me." When Fajgenbaum's Santa Claus theory collapsed, it also opened up space for a new belief system, one that would ultimately save his life.

Seeing the Obstacles and Solutions

Fajgenbaum now faced a choice that defines the difference between those who surrender to despair and those who find a way forward. He could accept the expert's pronouncements as final, sinking into the passive helplessness that claims so many facing terminal diagnoses. Or he could shift his perspective: If the answers weren't out there, perhaps he could help find them. What Fajgenbaum did mirrors a technique that Gabriele Oettingen calls *mental contrasting*: the deliberate pairing of future dreams with present obstacles.

Unlike magical thinking, mental contrasting doesn't indulge in perfect futures. It forces us to hold two things at once: the goal we desire and the barriers that make it difficult to achieve. Instead of indulging in fantasies of effortless success, our minds begin linking challenges with potential responses. Obstacles stop being reasons to quit; they become prompts for action.

Oettingen's research confirms that people who imagine both their goals and the obstacles in their way stick with their goals longer and achieve more. German university students who clearly visualized their target grades while also considering personal distractions and time constraints studied more diligently and performed better on exams.[12] Middle-aged adults who proactively paired their fitness or nutritional targets with awareness of internal temptations or scheduling conflicts followed through with their routines for far longer. With mental contrasting, obstacles automatically triggered solutions, even without conscious effort. What looks like a simple shift in thinking is actually a way of channeling the three powers that turn belief into action:

- **Attention:** Instead of filtering out obstacles, mental contrasting deliberately brings them into focus, creating a more complete and realistic picture of the challenge ahead.
- **Anticipation:** Mental contrasting creates expectations not just around success but also around the difficulties we'll need to overcome, preparing our minds and bodies for the effort required.

- **Agency:** Mental contrasting builds conviction in our capacity to handle obstacles rather than avoid them, strengthening the neural pathways that enable effective action under pressure.

Liberating beliefs don't simply make obstacles disappear. They help us see them more clearly and provide us with the tools to navigate through them. For Fajgenbaum, this shift was the difference between waiting and working. Instead of visualizing perfect health or trying to manifest a cure through positive thinking, he began systematically cataloging every barrier in his way: The only experimental drug for his disease had failed; no other treatments were in development; the world's leading expert had run out of options; his repeated relapses were becoming more severe and more frequent; he was approaching the lifetime maximum dose of chemotherapy.

Rather than becoming paralyzed by these obstacles or trying to wish them away, Fajgenbaum used them as a road map for action. Each barrier pointed to a problem that might be solved through research, collaboration, or creative thinking. The obstacles were no longer reasons to give up. They were clues to where breakthroughs might be possible.

With his body still weak from organ failure, Fajgenbaum worked twelve-hour days, methodically poring over a mountain of data, from medical records to tissue samples spanning his three and a half years of illness. He read immunology textbooks to understand the cellular mechanisms behind his symptoms. He searched medical databases for research that might provide even the faintest clue.

Fajgenbaum's analysis uncovered a connection no one had noticed. Two biomarkers surged months before every relapse, as though, in Fajgenbaum's words, "preparing for a fight even though there was no apparent threat": T-cell activation and VEGF, the protein behind blood vessel growth. Those surges likely drove the growth of his mysterious moles—the evidence doctors dismissed for years.

Looking back, Fajgenbaum realized the clues had been there all along. For years, doctors had noted unusual blood vessel growth in his lymph nodes, his retinas, and even within a benign colon polyp. But these observations had been scattered across different specialists, time frames, and medical contexts. No one had connected the dots because no one was looking.

Fajgenbaum's breakthrough began when he tried on the opposite of his beliefs, creating a portfolio of perspectives he could now choose from:

- Old belief: Stay focused on existing medical tests and established treatments.
  - New belief (the power of attention): Don't limit focus to standard approaches—pay attention to overlooked data points that reveal health patterns.

- Old belief: Medical experts have all the answers; patients just need to wait for the cures.
  - New belief (the power of anticipation): Experts don't have all the answers—expect progress to come through active patient-practitioner partnership.

- Old belief: A good patient follows directions.
  - New belief (the power of agency): A good patient doesn't just follow directions—they question, research, experiment with lifestyle changes, and contribute their own findings.

For Fajgenbaum, these changes in belief marked the end of waiting. What once appeared to be dead ends in his medical chart became new possibilities. The work ahead would be grueling, but he was no longer a bystander waiting for rescue.

The Cure Already on the Shelf

The final piece of Fajgenbaum's puzzle came from a medical school immunology lesson. A single biological switch called mTOR appeared to control both problems he'd identified: overactive immune cells and the blood vessel growth causing his skin moles. It was like tracing two glitches to one faulty circuit. One switch could explain the blood moles, the T-cell spikes, the organ failure, and the cycle of relapses. Block that switch, and the disease itself might stop.

Even more importantly, a drug already existed to block mTOR. Sirolimus, already approved by the FDA to prevent organ transplant rejection and sitting on pharmacy shelves for decades, had never been considered for Castleman disease. Fajgenbaum's research suggested it could hit both targets: immune system overactivation and VEGF-driven vessel growth.

By December 2013, a fifth relapse loomed. His body was failing again, and conventional treatments had nothing left to offer. There was no formal clinical trial underway, no established protocol, no expert consensus to lean on. What he had were his own medical data and sirolimus, an old drug used safely in transplant patients, that might also help his disease. It was a coherent story, and it pointed to a possible treatment. But coherence wasn't proof. It was a far cry from the kind of large-scale evidence physicians typically rely on. The risks were real.

Still, doing nothing meant certain decline. Fajgenbaum chose to act. His decision to try sirolimus wasn't driven by certainty—"There wasn't time to set up a formal clinical trial." It was driven by the determination to act despite uncertainty. He wasn't claiming he knew the outcome, nor was he pretending that positive thinking alone would carry him through. He acted because his beliefs had shifted from waiting for rescue to taking responsibility for his survival. That shift turned incomplete evidence into a plan, and paralysis into action.

"There has to be a first for everything," Fajgenbaum reasoned. "The fact that it hasn't been tried yet doesn't mean it won't work."

The bet paid off spectacularly. Fajgenbaum survived to marry his college sweetheart in 2014 and has now been in remission for over a decade, far beyond the single year that had been his longest previous remission.

Fajgenbaum's journey reveals a crucial truth about the connection between hope and action. "I think so often in life ... either you hope and pray or you take action. And I think ... they need to come together. They need to work in parallel."

Fajgenbaum's transformed beliefs about the patient-expert relationship became a model for revolutionizing medical research itself. Following his personal breakthrough, Fajgenbaum cofounded the Castleman Disease Collaborative Network, which brings together patients, researchers, and pharmaceutical companies to systematically identify new treatments for this rare disease. The organization operates on the principle that patients can actively help discover answers, rather than passively wait for them.

In 2022, he expanded that vision with Every Cure, an organization he cofounded that utilizes artificial intelligence to discover new applications for existing drugs, the very approach that saved him.

"Because over 80% of approved drugs are already generic, there's no profit incentive for drug companies to find new uses for them," Fajgenbaum explains.[13]

Every Cure's algorithms have already generated 66 million drug-disease compatibility scores, identifying possibilities that human researchers could never evaluate alone. This work represents belief change at a systems level—not waiting for medical breakthroughs to arrive, but actively designing conditions for breakthroughs to keep coming.

When Beliefs Work

Oftentimes, the ideas that feel most comforting do us the least good. It's easy to trust the promise that "everything will work out." But when it doesn't, we're left unprepared.

Beliefs that work focus our attention on what we can influence. They acknowledge challenges while building confidence in our ability to meet them. They channel hope into action, turning intention into concrete steps. They build capability over time, strengthening skills rather than substituting fantasy for effort. And because they operate through observable and measurable mechanisms, they help us see the world more clearly.

Beliefs that don't work promise control where none exists, setting us up for disappointment. They invite us to avoid obstacles instead of preparing for them. They replace effort with rehearsal, giving us the illusion of progress while leaving us less ready. They substitute wishful thinking for competence. And because they rely on forces that can't be tested, they pull us away from reality rather than deeper into it.

What set Fajgenbaum's story apart from so many others was how he harnessed the powers of belief. His belief helped him see what others missed. They prepared him to expect discovery rather than rescue. They gave him the courage to act when waiting meant decline.

We face the same choice between beliefs that empower us and those that limit us. And understanding this choice is the first step toward shaping the beliefs that will define our lives.

Rising Beyond Belief

The most resilient people, from entrepreneurs navigating volatile markets to healthcare workers managing clinical complexity to parents raising children in uncertain times, aren't those who avoid chaos. They're those who develop a different relationship with it, deploying all Three Powers of Belief in service of what matters most. They recognize that beliefs are not fixed truths. They are tools that can be adjusted, refined, or even discarded as life demands.

The shift from limiting to liberating beliefs doesn't happen through affirmations, vision boards, or magical rituals alone. It comes through direct experience and evidence of our ability to influence outcomes.

Anne Mahlum began with one morning run for nine men outside a homeless shelter, with the idea that a simple, shared routine could spark momentum and restore dignity. Daniel Gisler tested hypnosis on minor pains, with the belief that trained attention could blunt the agony of surgery. They didn't need perfect confidence before they took action. They required just enough belief to take the first small step and enough curiosity to let their results inform the acts that followed. Liberating beliefs emerge from liberating actions.

Which brings us to you.

As I finish writing this book, I can't help but think about life's bigger questions, the ones we rarely make time for until we're forced to confront them.

We get one life. One chance to leave our mark, to matter, to live according to what we truly value. Yet most days, it feels like we have forever. But all we really have is this moment, and the next, and the one after that. Each moment has the power to change everything—if we choose to act.

Think about the people in your life who inspire you most—not the famous names but the real people you know personally. What makes them memorable? It likely isn't the accomplishments on their résumé. It's how they live. They act with integrity even when no one is watching. They show up for the people they love. They take risks that matter. They choose growth over comfort. They allow themselves to be happy, even when the world gives them reasons not to be.

Now consider the opposite: the people you know who are filled with "what ifs" and "if onlys." They quit on relationships, projects, and themselves too soon. Overwhelmed, they make decisions guided by fear rather than possibility. They let pain and resentment steer their behavior. They have dreams and know what to do, but never find the courage to commit. They blame circumstances, "the world these days," or other people, while rarely taking action on the things they can do for themselves and others.

The difference between these two groups isn't talent, luck, or circumstances. It's belief. Specifically, it's whether they let limiting beliefs dictate their choices or challenge those beliefs and take action anyway.

I want you to think about your life—not just tomorrow or next week, but the arc of your entire existence. Ask yourself:

Attention: Where is your focus right now, and is it aligned with what truly matters to you? What have you refused to see about yourself, your relationships, or your life's path—because shifting your view feels uncomfortable? Could trying on the opposite belief reveal a "portfolio of perspectives"? Might one of those alternatives serve you better than the belief you're currently clinging to?

Anticipation: What future are you expecting for yourself, and who decided that path? Are you holding on to pain needlessly? How are you letting fear color your worldview? What becomes possible if you expect discovery instead of disappointment?

Agency: What's been holding you back? Are you letting life's invariable chaos energize you or drain you? Are you taking action to change yourself and help those around you, or are you waiting for the world to adjust to your liking? What is the one small step you could take today to prove to yourself that you have more control than you think?

Now imagine yourself at the end of your life. Picture the people gathered around you: family, friends, the ones who truly knew you. They reflect on how you lived and what you meant to them.

They speak of the way you stayed connected, how you mended what was broken, and how you chose to see the best in people. They talk about how you moved through the years with strength and vitality because you believed a long, healthy life was possible. They recall how you met even the hardest moments with the question of what good might still be made from them.

It is the kind of life people talk about with affection, the kind that makes them think, *I hope I get to live like that.* That is a rare life. One well lived.

That future begins long before the end. It starts with the beliefs you choose right here and now.

Soon you will close this book and begin the rest of your life with a clearer sense of what you are capable of. This transformation will not just change you; it will quietly influence the people around you. Your freedom from limiting beliefs will give others permission to question their own. Your small acts of agency will nudge someone else to take a first step. And your courage to live beyond what others expect will place you among the few who are remembered for how well they lived, the kind of person who stays in someone's heart and mind just like the people who inspire you.

The world will not get less chaotic. Uncertainty and setbacks will always be part of the story. But you have everything you need to move forward: the power to direct your attention, to anticipate possibility, and to take action despite unpredictability.

This is how David Fajgenbaum saved his own life when doctors said there was nothing more they could do. It's how Richter's rats swam for days when they believed escape was possible. It's how Dashrath Manjhi carved a road through a mountain with nothing but a hammer and a chisel.

None of them had certainty. All of them had belief.

Remarkable lives aren't built on grand declarations. They're built on persistent efforts—actions that create evidence, evidence that strengthens belief, and belief that fuels more action until possibility itself expands.

That is how you achieve extraordinary results.

That is how you live a life beyond belief.

FROM LIMITING BELIEFS...	TO LIBERATING BELIEFS...
I should avoid obstacles and setbacks because they indicate that I'm not succeeding.	Obstacles provide information that helps me navigate toward solutions.
Positive thinking alone will manifest my desires into reality.	Mental contrasting, which involves visualizing both goals and obstacles, facilitates the creation of actionable plans.
Someone else has the answers and will rescue me from my problems.	I can become an active participant in solving my own challenges.
Visualizing success is enough to achieve my goals.	Small actions create evidence that builds genuine confidence.
Prayer or manifestation will deliver results.	Hope and action must work together in parallel.

CHAPTER TAKEAWAYS

Chapter 1 Takeaways

The Power of Belief
- Beliefs are the foundation of motivation—without believing your efforts will matter, you'll quit well before reaching your potential.
- The Motivation Triangle consists of three elements: behavior (what to do), benefit (the desired outcome), and belief (the conviction that actions lead to results).
- Belief is more important than finding the "perfect" plan. Consistent action driven by conviction beats constantly switching strategies.

Beliefs Are Tools, Not Truths
- The most powerful beliefs aren't the ones you can prove beyond doubt—they're the ones that help you live better.
- Useful beliefs must withstand real-world feedback, stay open to revision, and engage honestly with evidence.
- Liberating beliefs should lead to action and growth, not wishes and fantasies.

Breaking the Quit Cycle
- Most failures happen because we quit too early, not because of flawed strategies or inevitable mistakes.
- The stories you tell yourself when giving up ("I'm not creative enough," "I'm not cut out for this," "This isn't me," "It's too late") aren't facts. They're limiting beliefs. Small, sustained changes

based on liberating beliefs beat dramatic overhauls that collapse when doubt creeps in.

The Three Powers of Belief Framework
- **Attention:** Believing is seeing. Your beliefs shape the opportunities and possibilities you notice.
- **Anticipation:** Beliefs act as emotional forecasts that influence your energy, mood, and performance.
- **Agency:** Beliefs give you a sense of control and turn intention into sustained action.

Practical Application
- Identify your limiting beliefs by listening to the whispers of doubt and self-criticism.
- Replace limiting beliefs with liberating ones that encourage action while staying grounded in reality.
- Treat belief-building like strength training—build beliefs through experience and evidence, not just positive thinking.

Chapter 2 Takeaways

The Power of Attention
- You see life through a keyhole. Your conscious mind processes only fifty bits of information per second out of eleven million bits your senses collect. Your brain doesn't passively record reality; it actively constructs your experience based on your beliefs.
- Two people can witness identical events and have completely different experiences because their beliefs filter what they notice.

Believing Is Seeing
- The saying "I'll believe it when I see it" is half the story—you actually see it when you believe it.
- Your beliefs determine what gets through your attentional filter and what gets ignored.
- Like optical illusions, you can know something intellectually but still perceive it inaccurately based on ingrained beliefs.

The Problem-Creation Trap
- As previous problems decrease, we unconsciously expand our definition of what constitutes a problem.
- If you expect to find threats, criticism, or failure, your brain will find evidence to support those beliefs—even when none exists.
- Rumination (repeatedly focusing on negative thoughts) strengthens neural pathways that keep you stuck.

The Power of Controlled Attention
- Like the hypnosedation patients who undergo surgery without anesthesia, you can learn to direct your attention away from what doesn't serve you.
- Attention is like a spotlight—whatever you shine it on becomes more noticeable.
- Changing your beliefs about what is possible can change what is actually possible for you.

Practical Application
- Recognize that your current problems may be partly created by where you're directing your attention.
- Practice deliberately looking for evidence that challenges your unhelpful beliefs.
- Use the third-person technique when you catch yourself spiraling into self-criticism ("Maria had a challenging day and is growing" vs. "I'm terrible" or "This is terrible").
- Ask, "Is thinking about this helping me improve or just making me feel worse?" Set time limits on rumination.
- Remember: We can reshape our perception of reality by directing our attention through the power of belief.

Chapter 3 Takeaways

The Perception Problem
- You don't have relationship problems—you have perception problems.
- The beliefs you hold about others determine what you're capable of seeing in them.
- Our closest relationships trigger automatic responses that bypass conscious control, causing us to revert to old patterns.

The Judgment Trap
- Once you form beliefs about someone, you automatically filter for confirming evidence while missing contradictory information.
- The longer you've known someone, the more you interact with your mental image of them rather than who they actually are.
- This creates self-fulfilling prophecies: Your beliefs → shape what you see → which influences how you act → which affects how others respond → which confirms your initial belief.

Four Questions to Examine Your Beliefs
(Adapted from Byron Katie's "The Work")
When upset about someone's behavior, ask yourself:

1. Is this belief true? (Recall your immediate judgment about a particular situation.)
2. Can I be certain this belief is true? (Look for even a small chance that another explanation could be true.)

3. How do I react when I believe this? (Notice the real consequences of this belief.)
4. Who would I be without this belief? (Imagine the same situation freed from your interpretation.)

Byron Katie's Turnaround Method
Turn your judgment around three ways and find genuine evidence for each:

- (To the Opposite) "She's too critical." → "She's not too critical."
- (To the Other) "She's too critical." → "I'm too critical of her."
- (To the Self) "She's too critical." → "I'm too critical of myself."

Building Your Portfolio of Perspectives
- Real change isn't trading one story for another. It's learning to see the same situation from many angles and choosing the one that serves you best.
- This gives you freedom to choose interpretations that serve connection rather than conflict.
- Cognitive flexibility means staying open to alternative explanations for someone's behavior.

Practical Application
- Start with minor irritations before tackling major relationship issues. For example, when wrestling with traffic, traveling through the airport, or dealing with a rude stranger.
- Keep a judgment journal—write down strong judgments and practice turning them around.
- Install *judgment alerts* for absolutist words like "always," "never," and "typical."

- Before reacting, imagine three non-negative explanations for someone's behavior.
- Listen for your strongest resistance to turnarounds—that's where the most growth lies.
- Remember: Your judgments about others reveal your own values, fears, and unmet needs.
- Transform relationships by changing your perception, without waiting for others to change.

Chapter 4 Takeaways

Your Beliefs Are Your Reality
- Your beliefs act as perceptual filters—they determine what opportunities, possibilities, and potential you notice or miss.
- *Belief-consistent information processing* means you seek evidence that confirms existing beliefs while filtering out contradictory information.
- Beliefs about transformation and potential train your mind to see possibilities where others see problems.
- Entrepreneurial alertness comes from beliefs that calibrate your attention to recognize patterns others miss.

Engineering Your Own Luck
- Lucky people don't experience more good fortune; they simply notice more opportunities by seeing the world from different perspectives.
- Luck favors those who step beyond the familiar—into new places, new people, and new experiences.
- Setting *failure goals* reframes rejection as data collection rather than defeat.
- Most breakthrough moments (60 to 88 percent) result from strategic actions that create conditions for luck to occur.

The Belief Blind Spot
- Your greatest strengths can become your greatest weaknesses when beliefs calcify into rigid thinking.

- Success reinforces existing beliefs, making you less receptive to feedback and more prone to blind spots.
- The conviction that fuels breakthroughs can prevent you from seeing needed changes.

Practical Application
- Regularly audit your beliefs: Which ones still open doors? Which might be quietly closing them?
- When receiving criticism, ask, "Could I be the problem?" rather than immediately attempting to defend yourself.
- Treat beliefs as upgradeable tools, not fixed truths or identity markers.
- Create systematic ways to disrupt your routine and expand what you notice.
- Practice seeing potential transformations in unexpected places and people. Remember that your perceptual filters are already running—choose them consciously rather than letting old programming run on autopilot.

Chapter 5 Takeaways

Your Brain Is a Prediction Machine
- Your subjective experience isn't delivered directly by your senses—it's your brain's best prediction about what your sensory input means.
- We live in personalized realities generated moment by moment, shaped by beliefs, memories, and expectations. Understanding this gives you the power to transform mundane moments into meaningful ones.

The Experience Loop: How Beliefs Become Your Reality
- **Step 1—Believe:** Your brain uses beliefs to create mental simulations of what's coming.
- **Step 2—Anticipate:** Your body physiologically prepares for the expected experience, adjusting your sensory processing.
- **Step 3—Feel:** You consciously interpret sensations through the lens of your expectations.
- **Step 4—Confirm:** You reinforce the original belief through reflection and social sharing.

Beliefs Drive Consumption
- We often want things purely because other people want them. Our brains use social signals as shortcuts to determine value.
- Successful brands don't just make what people want; they make people want what they make.

- The perception that "everyone wants this" triggers desire before conscious evaluation can intervene.

You Are a Simulation Designer
- Every expectation you set shapes how moments will feel before they arrive.
- Transform experiences by consciously reframing ordinary situations with different expectations.
- Great leaders design workplace "simulations" through the culture and narratives they create.

Practical Application
- Practice selective skepticism. Question beliefs that limit you or drain your energy and keep beliefs that add meaning, joy, or connection to your life.
- Before dreaded events, consciously set different expectations to change your experience.
- Use evocative language to transform ordinary offerings into anticipated experiences.
- Test your assumptions quickly and cheaply, rather than accepting limiting beliefs.
- Challenge negative anticipations that become self-fulfilling prophecies.
- Ask yourself: "Is this belief serving me, or am I serving it?"

Chapter 6 Takeaways

The Power of Anticipation
- Pain is created by your brain's predictions—identical physical stimuli produce different pain experiences based on what you expect.
- The brain has its own internal pharmacy that releases natural painkillers when you believe relief is on the way.
- Anticipatory anxiety worsens the perception of pain.

Motivation Is the Desire to Escape Discomfort
- We act to escape the discomfort of not acting.
- Procrastination is the avoidance of anticipated discomfort.
- Each time you avoid exercise, difficult conversations, or challenging work because you anticipate pain, you strengthen the neural association between that activity and negative feelings.

Breaking the Pain-Fear-Pain Cycle
- Neuroplastic pain persists when your brain predicts danger long after tissues heal.
- The cycle works like this: anticipate pain → feel fear → experience more pain → confirm danger.
- *Pain reprocessing therapy* breaks this cycle through observation (noticing without fear), safety reappraisal (looking for evidence that it's not dangerous), and positive affect (using levity to challenge predictions).

Placebos Without Deception
- Honest placebos work even when you know they're inert. Your conscious mind can understand that you've taken a placebo while your body responds as if it's medicine.
- Medicine distinguishes between illness (your subjective experience) and sickness (biological disease). Placebos dramatically improve how you feel without necessarily fixing underlying conditions.

Practical Application
- Reframe discomfort as "growth signals" rather than danger warnings.
- Create honest placebo rituals: Pair relief with consistent cues your brain can learn.
- Practice observing pain sensations with curiosity instead of catastrophic interpretation.
- Use movement and joy to prove to your brain that your body is safe.
- Remember that your physical experience isn't fixed—it's shaped moment to moment by what you expect to feel.

Chapter 7 Takeaways

The Biology of Belief
- Your beliefs about what your body can do become self-fulfilling prophecies through behavioral cascades that create biological transformations.
- Anticipation creates a chain reaction: Changing your expectations changes your behavior, which in turn changes your physical outcomes.
- Your body often possesses hidden capabilities that limiting beliefs keep locked away. Removing psychological constraints can reveal surprising potential.

Beyond Mind-Over-Matter Myths
- Beware of exaggerated claims about mindset alone transforming your body—many famous studies fail to replicate.
- Health-related beliefs work by unlocking motivation and effort, not by bypassing biology through pure thought.
- The most powerful belief changes happen when anticipation drives action, creating measurable improvements in strength, endurance, and performance.

Unlocking Hidden Potential
- Studies consistently show that altering perceptions of time, effort, or capability can enable performance beyond usual limits.

- Examples from Tibetan meditators generating body heat to Parkinson's patients displaying strength during sleep show that our bodies have untapped potential.
- Athletic research demonstrates that when psychological constraints are removed, people can access capabilities they didn't know they possessed.
- As Serena Williams's coach proved, sometimes "strategic deception" about your capabilities can unlock better performance by changing your beliefs.

The Aging Advantage
- Your beliefs about aging and physical capability literally influence your biology: People with positive aging beliefs live 7.5 years longer on average.
- How you think about aging affects how you age through multiple pathways: cognitive function, cardiovascular health, recovery ability, and preventive behaviors.
- Negative aging beliefs create avoidance cycles that lead to physical deconditioning, social isolation, and accelerated biological aging.
- Positive aging beliefs drive continued challenge-seeking, physical maintenance, and social engagement that slow the aging process.

Practical Application
- Notice the stories you tell yourself about what your body can and cannot do. These beliefs shape your physical reality over time.
- Embrace challenges that are appropriate to your current level while believing in your capacity for continued growth and adaptation.

- Build beliefs through evidence and experience: Start small, document improvements, and let success expand your sense of what's possible.
- Choose beliefs based on usefulness for driving positive behaviors, not just absolute truth—ask "Does this belief keep me going?"

Chapter 8 Takeaways

The Neuroscience of Agency
- Helplessness isn't learned—it's your brain's default response to uncontrollable situations, while agency must be actively developed through experience.
- Each time you successfully exert control in challenging situations, you strengthen neural pathways that can override passive responses.
- Your brain needs direct evidence that change is possible, not just positive thinking.

Life Is Chaos (and That's Normal)
- Feeling overwhelmed by chaos isn't a personal failure—it's proof you're fully alive in an inherently unpredictable world.
- The goal isn't to eliminate disorder but to develop a productive relationship with uncertainty.
- High-agency people don't expect fewer problems; they trust their ability to navigate whatever problems arise.

The Power of Internal Locus of Control
- An internal locus of control predicts better outcomes across all major life domains, including mental health, physical health, relationships, and career success.
- Focus on what you can control and influence while accepting genuine external constraints—this is *control flexibility*.

- Agency doesn't mean handling everything alone; it includes knowing when to ask for help and leverage resources.

The Stories You Tell Yourself
- Resilience grows when you see setbacks as temporary and specific, not permanent and global.
- Agency narratives highlight your meaningful choices and effective actions despite obstacles.
- Your *explanations* of past events, rather than the events themselves, shape your capacity for future action.

Practical Application
- Direct energy where you have the most leverage, rather than trying to control everything.
- Start with "optimal challenges"—tasks just beyond your comfort zone that provide proof your efforts matter.
- Create mastery experiences through graduated exposure to manageable difficulties.

Chapter 9 Takeaways

Prayer Works Through Psychology, Even Without Theology
- Prayer and ritual offer measurable psychological benefits, including reduced anxiety, enhanced emotional regulation, and increased resilience, regardless of one's theological certainty or spiritual beliefs.
- The brain responds to ritual through universal psychological mechanisms—what matters is engagement, not certainty.
- Research shows that people who pray regularly have thicker cerebral cortices, better stress responses, and greater endurance under pressure.

The Free Thinker Approach
- Free thinking means choosing practices based on evidence and personal benefit rather than unquestioning acceptance or complete rejection.
- Those who identify as "spiritual but not religious" often suffer the most, lacking structured practices to access transcendent experiences.
- *Constructive translation* lets you take part in spiritual traditions while maintaining intellectual integrity—interpreting religious language into something personally meaningful.

Five Universal Pathways from World Religions
- **Action before understanding:** Ritual practice shapes you even before you fully grasp its meaning. Start doing; understanding follows.

- **Submission to repetition:** Short, familiar rituals reset emotions and bring you back to what matters throughout the day.
- **Looking within:** Focus prayer inward on seeking truth and clarity about yourself, rather than requesting external changes.
- **Answering through community:** Prayer's power often manifests through human relationships and mutual support.
- **Transcending suffering:** Structured practices transform challenges into resilience, rather than attempting to eliminate difficulties.

The Power of Agency

- Agency transforms uncertainty into a bridge toward concrete benefits through intentional practice, even when perfect understanding remains elusive.
- You don't need certainty for prayer. You simply need willingness to engage with practices humans have found transformative for millennia.
- Secular rituals can be just as effective as religious ones when they incorporate repetition, structure, and meaningful symbolism.

Practical Application

- Start with simple, repeatable practices you can maintain daily, rather than elaborate rituals that require perfect conditions.
- Use prayer as structured problem-solving: Articulate your challenges clearly, form action plans, and separate what you can control from what requires acceptance.
- Build rituals into regular rhythms, such as morning routines or daily transitions, for consistent emotional regulation.

Chapter 10 Takeaways

The Danger of Nocebos
- The nocebo effect shows that negative beliefs create real physical symptoms. Expect harm, and your physiology can follow.
- Beliefs spread contagiously through groups and social media, amplifying fears and symptoms across entire communities.

The Identity Trap
- Diagnoses serve important purposes, but can become dangerous when they shift from descriptions to identities. ("I am challenged by anxiety at times" versus "I am an anxious person.")
- Identity foreclosure occurs when you prematurely commit to limiting labels, thereby closing off the exploration of your full potential.
- The language medical professionals use shapes beliefs. The label you hear shapes how you live with the condition.

When Help Becomes Harmful
- Well-intentioned therapeutic practices like trigger warnings and safe spaces can reinforce fragility rather than build resilience.
- Trauma-focused therapy can trap people in damage-centered narratives that make pain central to identity.
- Memory is a reconstruction, not a recording. The stories you tell about your past may be less permanent than you think.

Pills Don't Teach Skills

- Medication can provide crucial symptom relief but operates at the biochemical level, not the skill-building level.
- Overreliance on external solutions inhibits the development of internal capabilities and resilience.
- The best outcomes combine chemical interventions with therapy, skills training, and agency-building practices.

Practical Application

- Treat diagnoses as starting points for healing, not verdicts on your potential.
- Focus on building skills and capabilities alongside any treatments you receive.
- Avoid letting others' opinions become personal prophecy. Self-diagnoses can function as powerful nocebo suggestions.
- Question whether your beliefs and labels expand or contract your capacity to act effectively.
- Build agency through gradual exposure to discomfort rather than constant avoidance of triggers.

Chapter 11 Takeaways

The Negative Side of Positive Thinking
- Positive fantasies can backfire—they relax the body as if the goal were already achieved, draining energy for action.
- The Circle of False Promise traps people in cycles: Unfulfilled visualizations become evidence of personal failure, leading to deeper helplessness rather than empowerment.
- Magical thinking promises control where none exists, setting you up for disappointment when reality doesn't match fantasy.

Why Mental Contrasting Works
- Mental contrasting means deliberately pairing future dreams with present obstacles, creating automatic mental links between challenges and potential solutions.
- Unlike positive thinking, mental contrasting engages all Three Powers of Belief: directing attention to realistic obstacles, building anticipation for both success and difficulty, and strengthening agency to handle challenges.
- Obstacles stop being reasons to quit when you expect and plan for them.

The Santa Claus Theory
- Believing that experts have all the answers can create dangerous passivity, preventing you from developing your own understanding and taking necessary action.

- When authorities reach their limits, waiting for rescue becomes a recipe for helplessness rather than hope.
- The most empowering belief shift is from "someone else will solve this" to "I can contribute to finding solutions."

Building Beliefs Through Evidence
- Empowering beliefs emerge from empowering actions, not from positive affirmations or vision boards alone.
- Small successes build evidence of capability, gradually expanding what you believe is possible based on demonstrated competence.
- Each concrete step creates proof that strengthens belief, which fuels more action in an upward spiral.

Practical Application
- Practice mental contrasting by visualizing your desired outcome alongside the specific obstacles you are likely to face.
- Treat beliefs as navigation tools that can be updated based on new evidence rather than as absolute truths to defend.
- Focus on taking the next small step you can control rather than waiting for perfect conditions or external rescue.
- Remember that hope without action leads to false comfort, while action without hope leads to burnout—combine both for lasting progress.

Acknowledgments

Beyond Belief took five years to complete, and countless people deserve thanks for their contributions.

First and foremost, my deepest gratitude goes to my partner in business and life, Julie Li. Her contributions to this project are truly beyond belief. Julie spent countless hours editing, improving every chapter with her keen eye and thoughtful suggestions. She tested ideas with me, allowed me to share stories from our life, and walked this path by my side. She is my motivation and inspiration, and this book would not exist without her dedication and partnership.

To my daughter, Jasmine, who helped me think through many of the ideas in this book during our dinners and walks together. Her insights and questions often sparked new directions, and our many laughs over the silly ideas that didn't make it into the book are some of my favorite memories from this process.

To my parents, Victor and Ronit Eyal, and my in-laws, Anne and Paul Li, for always being my biggest supporters. I am especially grateful to my father, who was the very first to read my manuscript and whose thoughtful feedback and encouragement sustained me.

Special thanks to my friend Travis Sentell, who bravely read an early (and bad) version of this book, and whose friendship I continue to treasure.

I am deeply grateful to my longtime agent, Christy Fletcher, for more than seventeen years of guidance and unwavering belief in my work. I am also thankful to Sarah Fuentes and the entire team at UTA, with special thanks to Melissa Chinchillo, Georgie Melor, Yona Levin, Charlotte Perman, and Claire Yoo for their invaluable support over the years.

To my publishing partners: Niki Papadopoulos, my exceptional editor at Portfolio, deserves special recognition for her countless invaluable suggestions and thoughtful edits. Thank you, Niki, for being such a wonderful thought partner and champion of this work. I am also profoundly grateful to Adrian Zackheim, my publisher, for his faith in this book's mission and its potential to create meaningful change in people's lives. Special thanks to Leila Sandlin and Anna Dobbin, and to Paul Conner for his impeccable copyediting. In the UK, thank you to Geraldine Collard and Joel Rickett at Ebury, and to my UK agent, Cathryn Summerhayes.

To those who generously entrusted me with their stories and helped ensure I told them accurately: Anne Mahlum, Blair Braverman, Daniel Gisler, David Fajgenbaum, Hansruedi Wipf, and the religious leaders in Singapore who shared their wisdom.

David Moldawer deserves special recognition for his help in the project's early stages and for his patience as I found my footing. I am also grateful to Alexander Wieckowski, Juli Fraga, Maria Gagliano, Rob Goodman, and Seth Schulman for their editorial assistance, to Annie Graham for her research assistance—special thanks to Zofia Krajewska for her meticulous fact-checking and invaluable research support. Thank you to Zach Rubin and his colleagues for their focus group participation and insights.

Thank you to James Clear for his thoughtful help with positioning and titling this book.

To my beta readers—Andrew Sypkes, Ben Foster, Ben Gambrel, Cassius Kiani, George Sudo, Jeremy Shapiro, Marjorie, Matt Treacey, Rob Fitzpatrick, Ruby Ryba, Tristan, and Victoria—thank you for your invaluable feedback.

To those who helped with promotional efforts: Andrea Schumann, Ines Lee, Jinwei Lim, Jonathan Chua, and Karen Walpole.

I am indebted to the many scholars whose rigorous research I cite throughout these pages. Their work laid the foundation for this exploration of belief.

Finally, thank you, the reader, for spending your precious time with this book. It means the world to me. If I can be helpful, or if you have questions, please reach out at NirAndFar.com/contact.

If I have inadvertently overlooked anyone, I sincerely apologize. Please know the omission is not from lack of gratitude. As Hanlon's razor reminds us: "Never attribute to malice that which is adequately explained by stupidity." Thank you! Thank you! Thank you!

NOTES

Chapter 1. Beliefs Are Tools, Not Truths

1. Richter's full experimental protocol involved additional variables, including restraint, handling, and in some trials, trimming the rats' whiskers. Richter concluded that these stressors played "a contributory, rather than an essential, role" in the sudden-death response. The primary factor, in his analysis, was hopelessness—being in "a situation against which they have no defense." See Richter, C. P. (1957). On the phenomenon of sudden death in animals and man. *Psychosomatic Medicine*, 19(3), 191–198.

Chapter 2. Why Believing Is Seeing

1. Vanhaudenhuyse, A., Laureys, S., & Faymonville, M. E. (2014). Neurophysiology of hypnosis. *Neurophysiologie Clinique/Clinical Neurophysiology*, 44(4), 343–353. https://doi.org/10.1016/j.neucli.2013.09.006.

2. Badidi, G., Baulieu, M., Vercherin, P., De Pasquale, V., Gavid, M., & Prades, J. M. (2021). Thyroid surgery under hypnosis: A 50-case series. *European Annals of Otorhinolaryngology, Head and Neck Diseases*, 138(1), 13–17. https://doi.org/10.1016/j.anorl.2020.06.010.

3. Gisler, D. (January 8, 2025). Personal communication.

4. Korade, Z., & Mirnics, K. (2014). Programmed to be human? *Neuron*, 81(2), 224–226. https://www.ncbi.nlm.nih.gov/pmc/articles/PMC3950304.

5. Nørretranders, T. (1998). *The User Illusion: Cutting Consciousness Down to Size*. Viking.

6. Adelson, E. H. (1995). Checker shadow illusion. *Perceptual Science Group @ MIT*. http://persci.mit.edu/gallery/checkershadow.

7. Levari, D. E., Gilbert, D. T., Wilson, T. D., Sievers, B., Amodio, D. M., & Wheatley, T. (2018). Prevalence-induced concept change in human judgment. *Science*, 360(6396), 1465–1467. https://doi.org/10.1126/science.aap8731.

8. Gallup. (n.d.). Crime. *Gallup*. Retrieved April 2025, from https://news.gallup.com/poll/1603/crime.aspx.

9. Reuell, P. (June 28, 2018). We solved the problem! Now let's unsolve it. *Harvard Gazette*. https://news.harvard.edu/gazette/story/2018/06/harvard-researchers-may-have-answer-to-why-youre-never-satisfied.

10. Cooney, R. E., Joormann, J., Eugène, F., Dennis, E. L., & Gotlib, I. H. (2010). Neural correlates of rumination in depression. *Cognitive, Affective, & Behavioral Neuroscience*, 10(4), 470–478. https://doi.org/10.3758/CABN.10.4.470.

11. Hamilton, J. P., Farmer, M., Fogelman, P., & Gotlib, I. H. (2015). Depressive rumination, the default-mode network, and the dark matter of clinical neuroscience. *Biological Psychiatry*, 78(4), 224–230. https://doi.org/10.1016/j.biopsych.2015.02.020.

12. Connolly, S. L., Wagner, C. A., Shapero, B. G., Pendergast, L. L., Abramson, L. Y., & Alloy, L. B. (2014). Rumination prospectively predicts executive functioning impairments in adolescents. *Journal of Behavior Therapy and Experimental Psychiatry*, 45(1), 46–56. https://doi.org/10.1016/j.jbtep.2013.07.009.

13. Grossmann, I., Oakes, H., & Santos, H. C. (2019). Wise reasoning benefits from emodiversity, irrespective of emotional intensity. *Journal of Experimental Psychology*, 148(5), 805–823. https://psycnet.apa.org/doi/10.1037/xge0000543.

14. Kross, E., Bruehlman-Senecal, E., Park, J., Burson, A., Dougherty, A., Shablack, H., et al. (2014). Self-talk as a regulatory mechanism: How you do it matters. *Journal of Personality and Social Psychology*, 106(2), 304–324. https://doi.org/10.1037/a0035173.

15. Moser, J. S., Dougherty, A., Mattson, W. I., Katz, B., Moran, T. P., & Jarcho, J. M. (2017). Third-person self-talk facilitates emotion regulation without engaging cognitive control: Converging evidence from ERP and fMRI. *Scientific Reports*, 7, 4519. https://doi.org/10.1038/s41598-017-04047-3.

Chapter 3. The Secret to Better Relationships

1. Bushman, B. J. (2002), Does venting anger feed or extinguish the flame? Catharsis, rumination, distraction, anger, and aggressive responding, *Personality and Social Psychology Bulletin*, 28(6), 724–731, https://psycnet.apa.org/doi/10.1177/0146167202289002; Tavris, C. (1988), Beyond cartoon killings: Comments on two overlooked effects of television, in S. Oskamp (ed.), *Television as a Social Issue* (pp. 189–197), Sage Publications.

2. Ellis, A. (1962). *Reason and Emotion in Psychotherapy*. Lyle Stuart.

3. Keyes, K., Jr. (1975). *Handbook to Higher Consciousness*. Living Love Center.

4. Langer, E. J. (1989). *Mindfulness*. Addison-Wesley.

5. Levari, D. E., Gilbert, D. T., Wilson, T. D., Sievers, B., Amodio, D. M., & Wheatley, T. (2018). Prevalence-induced concept change in human judgment. *Science*, 360(6396), 1465–1467. https://doi.org/10.1126/science.aap8731.

6. Murray, S. L., Bellavia, G., Rose, P., & Griffin, D. W. (2003). Once hurt, twice hurtful: How perceived regard regulates daily

marital interactions. *Journal of Personality and Social Psychology*, 84(1), 126–147. https://doi.org/10.1037/0022-3514.84.1.126.

7. Katie, B., & Mitchell, S. (2002). *Loving What Is: Four Questions That Can Change Your Life*. Harmony Books.

8. Kashdan, T. B., & Rottenberg, J. (2010). Psychological flexibility as a fundamental aspect of health. *Clinical Psychology Review*, 30(7), 865–878. https://doi.org/10.1016/j.cpr.2010.03.001.

9. Smernoff, E., Mitnik, I., Kolodner, K., & Lev-ari, S. (2015). The effects of "The Work" meditation (Byron Katie) on psychological symptoms and quality of life—A pilot clinical study. *Explore: The Journal of Science and Healing*, 11(1), 24–31. https://doi.org/10.1016/j.explore.2014.10.003.

10. Ochsner, K. N., & Gross, J. J. (2005), The cognitive control of emotion, *Trends in Cognitive Sciences*, 9(5), 242–249, https://doi.org/10.1016/j.tics.2005.03.010; Gross, J. J. (2002), Emotion regulation: Affective, cognitive, and social consequences, *Psychophysiology*, 39(3), 281–291, https://doi.org/10.1017/s0048577201393198.

11. Edwards, K., & Smith, E. E. (1996), A disconfirmation bias in the evaluation of arguments, *Journal of Personality and Social Psychology*, 71(1), 5–24, https://doi.org/10.1037/0022-3514.71.1.5; Oeberst, A., & Imhoff, R. (2023), Toward parsimony in bias research: A proposed common framework of belief-consistent information processing for a set of biases, *Perspectives on Psychological Science*, 18(6), 1464–1487, https://doi.org/10.1177/17456916221148147.

Chapter 4. How to See Opportunities Others Miss

1. Facing the risk of failure, posted September 30, 2014, by CreativeMornings HQ. https://www.youtube.com/watch?v=JOBNLDn3WdA.

2. DeepCast. (2024). MoneyWise: From $175K to over $100M: Anne Mahlum's journey of all-in bets and astonishing success.

DeepCast. https://deepcast.fm/episode/from-175k-to-over-100m-anne-mahlums-journey-of-all-in-bets-and-astonishing-success.

3. How Anne Mahlum built and sold a $98m business: Lessons in scaling, leadership, and culture, posted December 6, 2024, by Jen Gottlieb. https://www.youtube.com/watch?v=K1hSIhe6UmE.

4. Letting go of complacency, posted September 12, 2016, by TEDx Talks. https://www.youtube.com/watch?v=kZbwlzhNrpg.

5. Running forward to alleviate homelessness: Anne Mahlum at TEDxAustin, posted February 19, 2013, by TEDx Talks. https://www.youtube.com/watch?v=LVWCqCe1D8Y.

6. Back on My Feet (2025). About us. Back on My Feet. https://backonmyfeet.org/about-us.

7. Baron, R. A. (2006). Opportunity recognition as pattern recognition: How entrepreneurs "connect the dots" to identify new business opportunities. *The Academy of Management Perspectives,* 20(1), 104–119. https://doi.org/10.5465/AMP.2006.19873412.

8. Wiseman, R. (2003). *The Luck Factor: Changing Your Luck, Changing Your Life: The Four Essential Principles.* Miramax Books.

9. Pasteur, L. (December 7, 1854). Inaugural lecture at the University of Lille, December 7, 1854.

10. Seelig, T. (2009). *What I Wish I Knew When I Was 20: A Crash Course on Making Your Place in the World.* HarperOne.

11. Le Bon, J. (April 13, 2015). Why the best salespeople get so lucky. *Harvard Business Review.* https://hbr.org/2015/04/why-the-best-salespeople-get-so-lucky.

12. Thier, J. (March 28, 2024). How the 43-year-old founder of [solidcore] made $100 million as her competitors went bankrupt. *Fortune.* https://fortune.com/2024/03/28/how-i-made-my-first-million-anne-mahlum-solidcore.

13. Sauer, M. (June 23, 2023). 42-year-old turned $175,000 into a Pilates company—then sold it for $88.4 million: "I put every dollar I had"

into it. *CNBC*. https://www.cnbc.com/2023/06/23/anne-mahlum-bet-life-savings-on-pilates-sold-solidcore-for-millions.html.

14. Kazemi, L. (June 7, 2021). [solidcore] explained. https://daofitlife.com/tools/solidcore-explained.

15. Mahlum, A. (February 4, 2025). Instagram post. https://www.instagram.com/annemahlum/p/DFqAG0XRGyj.

16. Facing the risk of failure, posted September 30, 2014, by CreativeMornings HQ. https://www.youtube.com/watch?v=JOBNLDn3WdA.

17. Baird, A. (August 15, 2020). Solidcore sells itself as an empowering fitness boutique. Employees say its CEO created a culture of toxicity and sexual harassment. *BuzzFeed News*. https://www.buzzfeednews.com/article/addybaird/solidcore-ceo-anne-mahlum-allegations-harassment.

18. [solidcore]. (April 18, 2023). [solidcore] founder Anne Mahlum sells her company, shares millions with employees. PR Newswire. https://www.prnewswire.com/news-releases/solidcore-founder-anne-mahlum-sells-her-company-shares-millions-with-employees-301800069.html.

Chapter 5. You Already Live in a Simulation

1. How Liquid Death's founder made water cool and became $700 million richer, posted November 8, 2022, by The Tom Ward Show. https://www.youtube.com/watch?v=g1ovWwZD_cU&t=2237s.

2. Connolly, B. (May 4, 2023). How Liquid Death turned water into a $1.4 billion brand & murdered the Amazon market. *JungleScout*. https://www.junglescout.com/resources/articles/liquid-death-amazon.

3. Frommer, D. (May 14, 2019). Liquid Death's founder explains his hardcore canned water startup. *The New Consumer*. https://newconsumer.com/2019/05/liquid-death-canned-water-brand-mike-cessario.

4. Why Liquid Death's branding sells—even though its water isn't special, posted December 12, 2024, by *The Wall Street Journal*. https://www.youtube.com/watch?v=UfpBPk8HiaY.

5. Nunn, J. F. (1996). *Ancient Egyptian Medicine*. University of Oklahoma Press.

6. Plato. (1901). *Phaedrus* (B. Jowett, trans.). In Plato & B. Jowett (trans.), *Dialogues of Plato: With Analyses and Introductions*, vol. 1, pp. 517–585. Charles Scribner's Sons.

7. Pinker, S. (1997). *How the Mind Works*. W. W. Norton & Company.

8. Moncrieff, J., Cooper, R. E., Stockmann, T., Amendola, S., Hengartner, M. P., & Horowitz, M. A. (2022). The serotonin theory of depression: A systematic umbrella review of the evidence. *Molecular Psychiatry*, 28, 3243–3256. https://doi.org/10.1038/s41380-022-01661-0.

9. Clark, A. (2013). Whatever next? Predictive brains, situated agents, and the future of cognitive science. *Behavioral and Brain Sciences*, 36(3), 181–204. https://doi.org/10.1017/s0140525x12000477.

10. Seth, A. (2021). *Being You: A New Science of Consciousness*. Faber and Faber.

11. Friston, K. (2010). The free-energy principle: A unified brain theory? *Nature Reviews Neuroscience*, 11(2), 127–138. https://doi.org/10.1038/nrn2787.

12. Girard, R. (1965), *Deceit, Desire, and the Novel: Self and Other in Literary Structure*, Johns Hopkins University Press; Girard, R. (1977), *Violence and the Sacred* (P. Gregory, trans.), Johns Hopkins University Press.

13. Plassmann, H., O'Doherty, J., Shiv, B., & Rangel, A. (2008). Marketing actions can modulate neural representations of experienced pleasantness. *Proceedings of the National Academy of Sciences*, 105(3), 1050–1054. https://doi.org/10.1073/pnas.0706929105.

14. Dawkins, L., Shahzad, F. Z., Ahmed, S. S., & Edmonds, C. J. (2011). Expectation of having consumed caffeine can improve performance and mood. *Appetite*, 57(3), 597–600. https://doi.org/10.1016/j.appet.2011.07.011.

15. Lee, C., Linkenauger, S. A., Bakdash, J. Z., Joy-Gaba, J. A., & Profitt, D. R. (2011). Putting like a pro: The role of positive contagion in golf performance and perception. *PLoS One*, 6(10), e26016. https://doi.org/10.1371/journal.pone.0026016.

16. Branthwaite, A., & Cooper, P. (1981). Analgesic effects of branding in treatment of headaches. *British Medical Journal (Clinical Research Ed.)*, 282(6276), 1576–1578. https://doi.org/10.1136/bmj.282.6276.1576.

17. Alexander, S. (March 1, 2022). Microaddictions. *Astral Codex Ten*. https://www.astralcodexten.com/p/microaddictions.

18. Associated Press. (July 2, 1993). Small factors keep Corolla rated higher than Prizm. *Deseret News*. https://www.deseret.com/1993/7/2/19054342/small-factors-keep-corolla-rated-higher-than-prizm.

19. Olive, S. E., Welti, T., & McMullin, E. (2013). Listener preferences for in-room loudspeaker and headphone target responses. *Audio Engineering Society Convention 134*, paper number 8867. http://www.aes.org/e-lib/browse.cfm?elib=16768.

20. Fraga, J. (January 20, 2024). Keeping a midlife crisis from wrecking your retirement plan. *New York Times*. https://www.nytimes.com/2024/01/20/business/midlife-crisis-retirement-savings.html.

Chapter 6. Sickness Is in the Body; Illness Is in the Mind

1. Healing story: Simon's journey healing their chronic widespread pain, posted December 3, 2024, by Tanner Murtaugh MSW, RSW. https://www.youtube.com/watch?v=sufyYo2uUVU.

2. Wager, T. D. (April 15, 2025). Re: Placebo response in neuroimaging studies [Email]. Personal communication.

3. Wager, T. D., Rilling, J. K., Smith, E. E., Sokolik, A., Casey, K. L., Davidson, R. J., et al. (2004). Placebo-induced changes in fMRI in the anticipation and experience of pain. *Science*, 303(5661), 1162–1167. https://doi.org/10.1126/science.1093065.

4. Wager, T., & Seago, L., What a pain in the brain!, *Like Mind, Like Body*, retrieved April 14, 2025, from https://www.curablehealth.com/podcast/mind-body-scientific-study-with-neuroscientist-dr-tor-wager; Wager, T. D., Scott, D. J., & Zubieta, J.-K. (2007), Placebo effects on human μ-opioid activity during pain, *Proceedings of the National Academy of Sciences*, 104(6), 11056–11061, https://doi.org/10.1073/pnas.0702413104.

5. Hutto, E. (November 15, 2022). Pain: The great motivator. *MedPage Today*. https://www.medpagetoday.com/painmanagement/painmanagement/101761.

6. Gilbert, D. T., & Wilson, T. D. (2000). Miswanting: Some problems in the forecasting of future affective states. In *The Construction of Preference* (Cambridge University Press), 550–564. https://doi.org/10.1017/CBO9780511618031.031.

7. Kross, E. (2021). *Chatter: The Voice in Our Head, Why It Matters, and How to Harness It*. Crown.

8. Giles, G. E., Cantelon, J. A., Eddy, M. D., Brunyé, T. T., Urry, H. L., Taylor, H. A., et al. (2018). Cognitive reappraisal reduces perceived exertion during endurance exercise. *Motivation and Emotion*, 42(4), 482–496. https://doi.org/10.1007/s11031-018-9697-z.

9. Brick, N. E., McElhinney, M. J., & Metcalfe, R. S. (2018). The effects of facial expression and relaxation cues on movement economy, physiological, and perceptual responses during running. *Psychology of Sport and Exercise*, 34, 20–28. https://doi.org/10.1016/j.psychsport.2017.09.009.

10. Gordon, A. (2021). *The Way Out: A Revolutionary, Scientifically Proven Approach to Healing Chronic Pain*. Avery.

11. Hashmi, J. A., Baliki, M. N., Huang, L., Baria, A. T., Torbey, S., Hermann, K. M., et al. (2013). Shape shifting pain: Chronification of back pain shifts brain representation from nociceptive to emotional circuits. *Brain*, 136(9), 2751–2768. https://doi.org/10.1093/brain/awt211.

12. Ashar, Y. K., Gordon, A., Schubiner, H., Uipi, C., Knight, K., Anderson, Z., et al. (2021). Effect of pain reprocessing therapy vs placebo and usual care for patients with chronic back pain: A randomized clinical trial. *JAMA Psychiatry*, 79(11), 13–23. https://doi:10.1001/jamapsychiatry.2021.2669.

13. Jonas, W. B. (2019), The myth of the placebo response, *Frontiers in Psychiatry*, 10, https://doi.org/10.3389/fpsyt.2019.00577; McGinnis, J. M., Williams-Russo, P., & Knickman, J. R. (2002), The case for more active policy attention to health promotion, *Health Affairs*, 21(2), 78–93, https://doi.org/10.1377/hlthaff.21.2.78.

14. Alcock, J. (2018). *Belief: What It Means to Believe and Why Our Convictions Are So Compelling*. Prometheus Books.

15. Wechsler, M. E., Kelley, J. M., Boyd, I. O., Dutile, S., Marigowda, G., Kirsch, I., et al. (2011). Active albuterol or placebo, sham acupuncture, or no intervention in asthma. *New England Journal of Medicine*, 365(2), 119–126. https://doi.org/10.1056/NEJMoa1103319.

16. Benedetti, F., & Dogue, S. (2015). Different placebos, different mechanisms, different outcomes: Lessons for clinical trials. *PLoS One*, 10, e0140967. https://doi.org/10.1371/journal.pone.0140967.

17. Moseley, J. B., O'Malley, K., Petersen, N. J., Menke, T. J., Brody, B. A., Kuykendall, D. H., et al. (2002). A controlled trial of arthroscopic surgery for osteoarthritis of the knee. *New England Journal of Medicine*, 347(2), 81–88. https://doi.org/10.1056/NEJMoa013259.

18. Kaptchuk, T. J., Friedlander, E., Kelley, J. M., Sanchez, M. N., Kokkotou, E., Singer, J. P., et al. (2010). Placebos without deception:

A randomized controlled trial in irritable bowel syndrome. *PLoS One*, 5, e15591. https://doi.org/10.1371/journal.pone.0015591.

19. Specter, M. (December 12, 2011). The power of nothing. *The New Yorker*. https://www.newyorker.com/magazine/2011/12/12/the-power-of-nothing.

20. Tuttle, A. H., Tohyama, S., Ramsay, T., Kimmelman, J., Schweinhardt, P., Bennett, G. J., et al. (2015). Increasing placebo responses over time in U.S. clinical trials of neuropathic pain. *Pain*, 156(12), 2616–2626. https://doi.org/10.1097/j.pain.0000000000000333.

21. Throw some ass/free the mind: How Sophie Hawley-Weld (SOFI TUKKER) beat chronic migraine & back pain. Posted November 5, 2024, by Curable Health. https://www.youtube.com/watch?v=rd6N6rtIv5U&ab_channel=CurableHealth.

22. Kaptchuk, T. J. (2018). Open-label placebo: Reflections on a research agenda. *Perspectives in Biology and Medicine*, 61(3), 311–334. https://doi.org/10.1353/pbm.2018.0045.

23. Benedetti, F., Pollo, A., Lopiano, L., Lanotte, M., Vighetti, S., & Rainero, I. (2003). Conscious expectation and unconscious conditioning in analgesic, motor, and hormonal placebo/nocebo responses. *Journal of Neuroscience*, 23(10), 4315–4323. https://doi.org/10.1523/jneurosci.23-10-04315.2003.

24. de Craen, A. J., Roos, P. J., de Vries, A. L., & Kleijnen, J. (1996). Effect of colour of drugs: systematic review of perceived effect of drugs and of their effectiveness. *BMJ*, 313(7072), 1624–1626.

25. Jacobs, K. W., & Nordan, F. E. (1979). Classification of placebo drugs: Effect of color. *Perceptual and Motor Skills*, 49(2), 367–372. https://doi.org/10.2466/pms.1979.49.2.367.

26. Zunhammer, M., Goltz, G., Schweifel, M., Stuck, B., & Bingel, U. (2022). Savor the flavor: A randomized double-blind study assessing taste-enhanced placebo analgesia in healthy volunteers. *Clinical and Translational Science*, 15(11), 2709–2719. https://doi.org/10.1111/cts.13397.

27. Vase, L., Robinson, M. E., Verne, G. N., & Price, D. D. (2005). Increased placebo analgesia over time in irritable bowel syndrome (IBS) patients is associated with desire and expectation but not endogenous opioid mechanisms. *Pain*, 115(3), 338–347. https://doi.org/10.1016/j.pain.2005.03.014.

28. Colloca, L., & Benedetti, F. (2005). Placebos and painkillers: Is mind as real as matter? *Nature Reviews Neuroscience*, 6, 545–552. https://doi.org/10.1038/nrn1705.

Chapter 7. Living Longer, Stronger, and Smarter

1. Lee, S. W. (August 23, 2021). The granfluencers: Team Strong Silvers. *The UrbanWire*. https://theurbanwire.sg/the-granfluencers-team-strong-silvers.

2. Malone, D. (1981). *The Sage of Monticello: Jefferson and His Time*, vol. 6. Little, Brown and Company.

3. McCullough, D. (2001). *John Adams*. Simon & Schuster.

4. Phillips, D. P., & Smith, D. G. (1990), Postponement of death until symbolically meaningful occasions, *JAMA*, 263(14), 1947–1951; Phillips, D. P., & King, E. W. (1988), Death takes a holiday: Mortality surrounding major social occasions, *The Lancet*, 2(8613), 728–732, https://doi.org/10.1016/s0140-6736(88)90198-5.

5. Langer, E. J. (1990). Old age: An artifact? In C. N. Alexander & E. J. Langer, eds., *Higher Stages of Human Development: Perspectives on Adult Growth* (pp. 222–240). Oxford University Press.

6. Crum, A. J., & Langer, E. J. (2007). Mind-set matters: Exercise and the placebo effect. *Psychological Science*, 18(2), 165–171. https://doi.org/10.1111/j.1467-9280.2007.01867.x.

7. Crum, A. J., Corbin, W. R., Brownell, K. D., & Salovey, P. (2011). Mind over milkshakes: Mindsets, not just nutrients, determine ghrelin response. *Health Psychology*, 30(4), 424–429. https://doi.org/10.1037/a0023467.

8. Open Science Collaboration (2015). Estimating the reproducibility of psychological science. *Science*, 349(6251), aac4716. https://doi.org/10.1126/science.aac4716.

9. Stanforth, D., Steinhardt, M., Mackert, M., Stanforth, P. R., & Gloria, C. T. (2011). An investigation of exercise and the placebo effect. *American Journal of Health Behavior*, 35(3), 257–268. https://doi.org/10.5993/ajhb.35.3.1.

10. Boardwalk Pictures, Delirio Films, & SpringHill Entertainment (2020). *The Playbook* [series]. Netflix. https://www.netflix.com/title/81025735.

11. Ariel, G., & Saville, W. (1972). Anabolic steroids: The physiological effects of placebos. *Medicine and Science in Sports and Exercise*, 4(2), 124–126.

12. Ross, M., & Olson, J. M. (1981). An expectancy-attribution model of the effects of placebos. *Psychological Review*, 88(5), 408–437.

13. Rozenkrantz, L., Mayo, A. E., Ilan, T., Hart, Y., Noy, L., & Alon, U. (2017). Placebo can enhance creativity. *PLoS One*, 12, e0182466. https://doi.org/10.1371/journal.pone.0182466.

14. Turi, Z., Mittner, M., Paulus, W., & Antal, A. (2017). Placebo intervention enhances reward learning in healthy individuals. *Scientific Reports*, 8, 41028. https://doi.org/10.1038/srep41028.

15. Kwon, D. (2022). Acting out dreams predicts Parkinson's and other brain diseases. *Scientific American*, 328(2), 56. https://www.scientificamerican.com/article/acting-out-dreams-predicts-parkinsons-and-other-brain-diseases.

16. Kozhevnikov, M., Elliott, J., Shephard, J., & Gramann, K. (2013). Neurocognitive and somatic components of temperature increases during g-tummo meditation: Legend and reality. *PLoS One*, 8, e58244. https://doi.org/10.1371/journal.pone.0058244.

17. Benson, H., Lehmann, J. W., Malhotra, M. S., Goldman, R. F., Hopkins, J., & Epstein, M. D. (1982). Body temperature changes

during the practice of g Tum-mo yoga. *Nature*, 295, 234–236. https://doi.org/10.1038/295234a0.

18. Osterhout, J. A., Kapoor, V., Eichhorn, S. W., Vaughn, E., Moore, J. D., Liu, D., et al. (2022). A preoptic neuronal population controls fever and appetite during sickness. *Nature*, 606, 937–944. https://doi.org/10.1038/s41586-022-04793-z.

19. Draganich, C., & Erdal, K. (2014). Placebo sleep affects cognitive functioning. *Journal of Experimental Psychology: Learning, Memory, and Cognition*, 40(3), 857–864. https://doi.org/10.1037/a0035546.

20. Morton, R. H. (2009). Deception by manipulating the clock calibration influences cycle ergometer endurance time in males. *Journal of Science and Medicine in Sport*, 12(2), 332–337. https://doi.org/10.1016/j.jsams.2007.11.006.

21. Stone, M. R., Thomas, K., Wilkinson, M., Jones, A. M., St Clair Gibson, A., & Thompson, K. G. (2012). Effects of deception on exercise performance: Implications for determinants of fatigue in humans. *Medicine and Science in Sports and Exercise*, 44(3), 534–541. https://doi.org/10.1249/mss.0b013e318232cf77.

22. Levy, B. R., Slade, M. D., Kunkel, S. R., & Kasl, S. V. (2002). Longevity increased by positive self-perceptions of aging. *Journal of Personality and Social Psychology*, 83(2), 261–270. https://doi.org/10.1037//0022-3514.83.2.261.

23. Levy, B. R., Pilver, C., Chung, P. H., & Slade, M. D. (2014). Subliminal strengthening: Improving older individuals' physical function over time with an implicit-age-stereotype intervention. *Psychological Science*, 25(12), 2127–2135. https://doi.org/10.1177/0956797614551970.

24. Levy, B. (1996), Improving memory in old age through implicit self-stereotyping, *Journal of Personality and Social Psychology*, 71(6), 1092–1107, https://psycnet.apa.org/doi/10.1037/0022-3514.71.6.1092; Levy, B. R., Zonderman, A. B., Slade, M. D., & Ferrucci, L. (2012), Memory shaped by age stereotypes over time, *Journals of*

Gerontology: Series B, Psychological Sciences and Social Sciences, 67(4), 432–436.

25. Levy, B. R., Hausdorff, J. M., Hencke, R., & Wei, J. Y. (2000). Reducing cardiovascular stress with positive self-stereotypes of aging. *The Journals of Gerontology Series B: Psychological Sciences and Social Sciences,* 55(4), P205–P213. https://doi.org/10.1093/geronb/55.4.P205.

26. Levy, B. R., Slade, M. D., Murphy, T. E., & Gill, T. M. (2012). Association between positive age stereotypes and recovery from disability in older persons. *JAMA,* 308(19), 1972–1973. https://doi.org/10.1001/jama.2012.14541.

27. Levy, B. R., & Myers, L. M. (2004). Preventive health behaviors influenced by self-perceptions of aging. *Preventive Medicine,* 39(3), 625–629. https://doi.org/10.1016/j.ypmed.2004.02.029.

28. Levy, B. R., Slade, M. D., Zonderman, A. B., & Ferrucci, L. (2009). Age stereotypes held earlier in life predict cardiovascular events in later life. *Psychological Science,* 20(3), 296–298. https://doi.org/10.1111/j.1467-9280.2009.02298.x.

Chapter 8. How to Take Control of Your Life (Even When It's Impossible)

1. Davies, D. (November 16, 2021). Iditarod sled dog musher Blair Braverman shares tales from the trail. NPR: *Fresh Air.* https://www.npr.org/transcripts/1055933800.

2. Overmier, J. B., & Seligman, M. E. P. (1967). Effects of inescapable shock upon subsequent escape and avoidance responding. *Journal of Comparative and Physiological Psychology,* 63(1), 28–33. https://psycnet.apa.org/doi/10.1037/h0024166.

3. Seligman, M. E., & Maier, S. F. (1967). Failure to escape traumatic shock. *Journal of Experimental Psychology,* 74(1), 1–9. https://psycnet.apa.org/doi/10.1037/h0024514.

4. Maier, S. F., & Seligman, M. E. P. (2016). Learned helplessness at fifty: Insights from neuroscience. *Psychological Review*, 123(4), 349–367. https://doi.org/10.1037/rev0000033.

5. Seligman, M. E. P. (2018). *The Hope Circuit: A Psychologist's Journey from Helplessness to Optimism*. Public Affairs.

6. Hauner, K. K., Mineka, S., Voss, J. L., & Paller, K. A. (2012). Exposure therapy triggers lasting reorganization of neural fear processing. *Proceedings of the National Academy of Sciences*, 109(23), 9203–9208. https://doi.org/10.1073/pnas.1205242109.

7. Craske, M. G., Treanor, M., Conway, C. C., Zbozinek, T., & Vervliet, B. (2014). Maximizing exposure therapy: An inhibitory learning approach. *Behaviour Research and Therapy*, 58, 10–23. https://doi.org/10.1016/j.brat.2014.04.006.

8. Braverman, B. (August 1, 2017). How to keep your cool, no matter what. *Outside*. https://www.outsideonline.com/culture/active-families/lost-art-keeping-cool-head.

9. Schrödinger, E. (1944). *What Is Life? The Physical Aspect of the Living Cell*. Cambridge University Press.

10. Kauffman, S. (2000). *Investigations*. Oxford University Press.

11. Churnin, N. (2017). *Manjhi Moves a Mountain*. Creston Books.

12. Rotter, J. B. (1966). Generalized expectancies for internal versus external control of reinforcement. *Psychological Monographs: General and Applied*, 80(1), 1–28. https://psycnet.apa.org/doi/10.1037/h0092976.

13. Kahana, B., Harel, Z., & Kahana, E. (2015). *Holocaust Survivors and Immigrants: Late Life Adaptations*. Springer.

14. Lachman, M. E., & Weaver, S. L. (1998). The sense of control as a moderator of social class differences in health and well-being. *Journal of Personality and Social Psychology*, 74(3), 763–773. https://doi.org/10.1037//0022-3514.74.3.763.

15. Gale, C. R., Batty, G. D., & Deary, I. J. (2008). Locus of control at age 10 years and health outcomes and behaviors at age 30 years: The 1970 British Cohort Study. *Psychosomatic Medicine*, 70(4), 397–403. https://doi.org/10.1097/psy.0b013e31816a719e.

16. Wrzus, C., Hänel, M., Wagner, J., & Neyer, F. J. (2013), Social network changes and life events across the life span: A meta-analysis, *Psychological Bulletin*, 139(1), 53–80, https://doi.org/10.1037/a0028601; Lad, T. P., & Kakulte, A. T. (2022), Locus of control, dyadic coping and relationship satisfaction: A correlational study in married couples, *EAS Journal of Psychology and Behavioural Sciences*, 4(1), 15–23.

17. Thoits, P. A. (2011). Mechanisms linking social ties and support to physical and mental health. *Journal of Health and Social Behavior*, 52(2), 145–161. https://doi.org/10.1177/0022146510395592.

18. Furnham, A., & Cheng, H. (2017). Socio-demographic indicators, intelligence, and locus of control as predictors of adult financial well-being. *Journal of Intelligence*, 5(2), 11. https://doi.org/10.3390/jintelligence5020011.

19. Hamzah, M. I., & Othman, A. K. (2022), How do locus of control influence business and personal success? The mediating effects of entrepreneurial competency, *Frontiers in Psychology*, 13, 958911, https://doi.org/10.3389/fpsyg.2022.958911; Kiprotich, S., & Kiprotich, J. (2023), The influence of internal locus of control and entrepreneurial skills on the growth of micro and small enterprises in Bomet County, Kenya, *Journal of Entrepreneurship & Project Management*, 3(1), 1–14, https://doi.org/10.70619/vol3iss1pp1-14.

20. Yeager, D. S., Hanselman, P., Walton, G. M., Murray, J. S., Crosnoe, R., Muller, C., et al. (2019). A national experiment reveals where a growth mindset improves achievement. *Nature*, 573, 364–369. https://doi.org/10.1038/s41586-019-1466-y.

21. Cheng, C., Cheung, S. F., Chio, J. H., & Chan, M. P. (2013). Cultural meaning of perceived control: A meta-analysis of locus of control and psychological symptoms across 18 cultural regions.

Psychological Bulletin, 139(1), 152–188. https://doi.org/10.1037/a0028596.

22. Chang, A. (March 21, 2019). Blair Braverman and her dogs finish first attempt at Iditarod. NPR: *All Things Considered*. https://www.npr.org/2019/03/21/705594646/blair-braverman-and-her-dogs-finish-first-attempt-at-iditarod.

23. Mealer, M., Jones, J., & Moss, M. (2012). A qualitative study of resilience and posttraumatic stress disorder in United States ICU nurses. *Intensive Care Medicine*, 38(9), 1445–1451. https://doi.org/10.1007/s00134-012-2600-6.

24. McAdams, D. P., Reynolds, J., Lewis, M., Patten, A. H., & Bowman, P. J. (2013), When bad things turn good and good things turn bad: Sequences of redemption and contamination in life narrative and their relation to psychosocial adaptation in midlife adults and in students, *Personality and Social Psychology Bulletin*, 27(4), 474–485, https://psycnet.apa.org/doi/10.1177/0146167201274008; McAdams, D. P., & McLean, K. C. (2013), Narrative identity, *Current Directions in Psychological Science*, 22(3), 233–238, https://doi.org/10.1177/0963721413475622; Adler, J. M. (2012), Living into the story: Agency and coherence in a longitudinal study of narrative identity development and mental health over the course of psychotherapy, *Journal of Personality and Social Psychology*, 102(2), 367–389, https://doi.org/10.1037/a0025289.

25. Johnson, C. G. (April 9, 2015). 30 years on death row: A conversation with Anthony Ray Hinton. *The Marshall Project*. https://www.themarshallproject.org/2015/04/09/30-years-on-death-row-a-conversation-with-anthony-ray-hinton.

26. Neal, D. T., Wood, W., & Drolet, A. (2012). How do people adhere to goals when willpower is low? The profits (and pitfalls) of strong habits. *Journal of Personality and Social Psychology*, 104(6), 959–975. https://doi.org/10.1037/a0032626.

Chapter 9. Prayer Works, With or Without Faith

1. Miller, L., Wickramaratne, P., Gameroff, M. J., Sage, M., Tenke, C. E., & Weissman, M. M. (2011). Religiosity and major depression in adults at high risk: A ten-year prospective study. *American Journal of Psychiatry*, 169(1), 89–98. https://doi.org/10.1176/appi.ajp.2011.10121823.

2. Tartaro, J., Luecken, L. J., & Gunn, H. E. (2005). Exploring heart and soul: Effects of religiosity/spirituality and gender on blood pressure and cortisol stress responses. *Journal of Health Psychology*, 10(6), 753–766. https://doi.org/10.1177/1359105305057311.

3. Lazar, S. W., Kerr, C. E., Wasserman, R. H., Gray, J. R., Greve, D. N., Treadway, M. T., et al. (2005). Meditation experience is associated with increased cortical thickness. *Neuroreport*, 16(17), 1893–1897. https://doi.org/10.1097/01.wnr.0000186598.66243.19.

4. Wachholtz, A. B., & Pargament, K. I. (2005). Is spirituality a critical ingredient of meditation? Comparing the effects of spiritual meditation, secular meditation, and relaxation on spiritual, psychological, cardiac, and pain outcomes. *Journal of Behavioral Medicine*, 28(4), 369–384. https://doi.org/10.1007/s10865-005-9008-5.

5. Shimron, Y. (May 26, 2021). Study: More churches closing than opening. *Religion News Service*. https://religionnews.com/2021/05/26/study-more-churches-closing-than-opening.

6. Pew Research Center (2018), Attitudes toward spirituality and religion, in *Being Christian in Western Europe*, https://www.pewresearch.org/religion/2018/05/29/attitudes-toward-spirituality-and-religion; Alper, B. A., Rotolo, C., Tevington, P., Nortey, J., & Kallo, A. (2023), Spirituality among Americans, Pew Research Center, https://www.pewresearch.org/religion/2023/12/07/spirituality-among-americans.

7. King, M., Marston, L., McManus, S., Brugha, T., Meltzer, H., & Bebbington, P. (2013). Religion, spirituality and mental health:

Results from a national study of English households. *The British Journal of Psychiatry*, 202(1), 68–73. https://doi.org/10.1192/bjp.bp.112.112003.

8. Ano, G. G., & Vasconcelles, E. B. (2005). Religious coping and psychological adjustment to stress: A meta-analysis. *Journal of Clinical Psychology*, 61(4), 461–480. https://doi.org/10.1002/jclp.20049.

9. Xygalatas, D. (2022). *Ritual: How Seemingly Senseless Acts Make Life Worth Living*. Little, Brown Spark.

10. Schille-Hudson, E. (January 9, 2025), The power of prayer: Praying is a cognitive practice full of problem-solving resources, *Aeon*, https://aeon.co/essays/why-prayer-is-a-problem-solving-practice-that-works; Iles-Caven, Y., Gregory, S., Ellis, G., Golding, J., & Nowicki, S. (2020), The relationship between locus of control and religious behavior and beliefs in a large population of parents: An observational study, *Frontiers in Psychology*, 11, Article 1462, https://doi.org/10.3389/fpsyg.2020.01462.

11. Al-Bukhārī. (n.d.). *Ṣaḥīḥ al-Bukhārī*, Hadith 39. As cited in Elias, A. A. (April 30, 2011). Islam is easy and religion is not to be made difficult. Daily Hadith Online. https://www.abuaminaelias.com/dailyhadithonline/2011/04/30/islam-is-easy.

12. Bormann, J. E., Smith, T. L., Becker, S., Gershwin, M., Pada, L., Grudzinski, A. H., et al. (2005). Efficacy of frequent mantram repetition on stress, quality of life, and spiritual well-being in veterans: A pilot study. *Journal of Holistic Nursing*, 23(4), 395–414. https://doi.org/10.1177/0898010105278929.

13. Durkheim, E. (2008). *The Elementary Forms of Religious Life*. Oxford University Press.

14. Porges, S. W. (2011). *The Polyvagal Theory: Neurophysiological Foundations of Emotions, Attachment, Communication, and Self-Regulation*. W. W. Norton & Company.

15. Holt-Lunstad, J., Smith, T. B., Baker, M., Harris, T., & Stephenson, D. (2015). Loneliness and social isolation as risk

factors for mortality: A meta-analytic review. *Perspectives on Psychological Science*, 10(2), 227–237. https://doi.org/10.1177/1745691614568352.

16. Bensen, G. (June 19, 2023). Personal communication.

17. Xygalatas, D. (2022). *Ritual: How Seemingly Senseless Acts Make Life Worth Living*. Little, Brown Spark.

18. Smietana, B. (September 24, 2021). The Sunday Assembly hopes to organize a godless future. It's not easy. *Religion News Service*. https://religionnews.com/2021/09/24/the-sunday-assembly-hopes-to-organize-a-godless-future-its-not-easy.

19. American Ethical Union. Member societies. https://aeu.org/who-we-are/member-societies.

20. Humanists International (December 19, 2022). European Humanist Federation dissolves. https://humanists.international/2022/12/european-humanist-federation-dissolved.

Chapter 10. Your Labels Are Your Limits

1. Reeves, R. R., Ladner, M. E., Hart, R. H., & Burke, R. S. (2007). Nocebo effects with antidepressant clinical drug trial placebos. *General Hospital Psychiatry*, 29(3), 275–277. https://doi.org/10.1016/j.genhosppsych.2007.01.010.

2. Palese, A., Rossettini, G., Colloca, L., & Testa, M. (2019). The impact of contextual factors on nursing outcomes and the role of placebo/nocebo effects: A discussion paper. *Pain Reports*, 4(3), e716. https://doi.org/10.1097/PR9.0000000000000716.

3. Faasse, K., & Petrie, K. J. (2013). The nocebo effect: Patient expectations and medication side effects. *Postgraduate Medical Journal*, 89(1055), 540–546. https://doi.org/10.1136/postgradmedj-2012-131730.

4. Blasini, M., Corsi, N., Klinger, R., & Colloca, L. (2017). Nocebo and pain: An overview of the psychoneurobiological

mechanisms. *Pain Reports*, 2(2), e585. https://doi.org/10.1097/pr9.0000000000000585.

5. Metzger, F. C. (1947). Emotions in the allergic individual. *American Journal of Psychiatry*, 103(5), 697–699. https://doi.org/10.1176/ajp.103.5.697.

6. Better Health Channel (July 23, 2021), Placebo effect, Department of Health, State Government of Victoria, https://www.betterhealth.vic.gov.au/health/conditionsandtreatments/placebo-effect; Hovav, K. (April 3, 2023), Unwanted side effects? The nocebo effect may be to blame, GoodRx, https://www.goodrx.com/health-topic/mental-health/nocebo-effect.

7. Wartolowska, K. (2019). The nocebo effect as a source of bias in the assessment of treatment effects. *F1000Research*, 8, 5. https://doi.org/10.12688/f1000research.17611.2.

8. Enck, P., Benedetti, F., & Schedlowski, M. (2008), New insights into the placebo and nocebo responses, *Neuron*, 59(2), 195–206, https://doi.org/10.1016/j.neuron.2008.06.030; Petrie, K. J., & Rief, W. (2019), Psychobiological mechanisms of placebo and nocebo effects: Pathways to improve treatments and reduce side effects, *Annual Review of Psychology*, 70, 599–625, https://doi.org/10.1146/annurev-psych-010418-102907.

9. Benedetti, F., Carlino, E., & Pollo, A. (2011), How placebos change the patient's brain, *Neuropsychopharmacology*, 36(1), 339–354, https://doi.org/10.1038/npp.2010.81; Colloca, L., & Benedetti, F. (2007), Nocebo hyperalgesia: How anxiety is turned into pain, *Current Opinion in Anesthesiology*, 20(5), 435–439, https://doi.org/10.1097/aco.0b013e3282b972fb.

10. Fielding, J. W., Fagg, S. L., Jones, B. G., Ellis, D., Hockey, M.S., Minawa, A., et al. (1983), An interim report of a prospective, randomized, controlled study of adjuvant chemotherapy in operable gastric cancer: British Stomach Cancer Group, *World Journal of Surgery*, 7(3), 390–399, https://doi.org/10.1007/BF01658089; Monvoisin, R., & Pinsault, N. (April 2019), First, do no harm,

Le Monde diplomatique, https://mondediplo.com/2019/04/09placebos.

11. Kleck, R. E., & Strenta, A. (1980). Perceptions of the impact of negatively valued physical characteristics on social interaction. *Journal of Personality and Social Psychology*, 39(5), 861–873. https://psycnet.apa.org/doi/10.1037/0022-3514.39.5.861.

12. Costa, A., Jesus, S., Almeida, M., & Alcafache, J. (2022). Psychogenic epidemic—mass hysteria phenomena in Portugal. *European Psychiatry*, 65(S1), S395. https://doi.org/10.1192/j.eurpsy.2022.999.

13. Moss, P. D., & McEvedy, C. P. (1966). An epidemic of overbreathing among schoolgirls. *British Medical Journal*, 2(5525), 1295–1300. https://doi.org/10.1136/bmj.2.5525.1295.

14. Dzokoto, V. A., & Adams, G. (2005). Understanding genital-shrinking epidemics in West Africa: Koro, juju, or mass psychogenic illness? *Culture, Medicine and Psychiatry*, 29(1), 53–78. https://doi.org/10.1007/s11013-005-4623-8.

15. Banerji, R. (May 30, 2016). Peruvian school kids claiming to be possessed by a demon have got the world completely baffled. *India Times*. https://www.indiatimes.com/culture/who-we-are/peruvian-school-kids-claiming-to-be-possessed-by-a-demon-have-got-the-world-completely-baffled-255747.html.

16. Corzine, T., & Roy, A. (2024). Inside the black mirror: Current perspectives on the role of social media in mental illness self-diagnosis. *Discover Psychology*, 4(40). https://doi.org/10.1007/s44202-024-00152-3.

17. Ricono, A., & Fahrlander, C. (June 16, 2022). 'I knew I was dying': How 5 rounds of Narcan possibly saved KCK police officer's life. *KCTV5 News*. https://www.kctv5.com/2022/06/16/i-knew-i-was-dying-how-5-rounds-narcan-possibly-saved-kck-police-officers-life.

18. Bach, R. (1977). *Illusions: The Adventures of a Reluctant Messiah*. Dell Publishing.

19. Marcia, J. E. (1966). Development and validation of ego-identity status. *Journal of Personality and Social Psychology*, 3(5), 551–558. https://psycnet.apa.org/doi/10.1037/h0023281.

20. Altmann, B., Fleischer, K., Tse, J., & Haslam, N. (2024), Effects of diagnostic labels on perceptions of marginal cases of mental ill-health, *PLOS Mental Health*, 1(3), e0000096, https://doi.org/10.1371/journal.pmen.0000096; Mehta, S., & Farina, A. (1997), Is being "sick" really better? Effect of the disease view of mental disorder on stigma, *Journal of Social and Clinical Psychology*, 16(4), 405–419, http://dx.doi.org/10.1521/jscp.1997.16.4.405.

21. Frick, M. A., Brandt, A., Hellund, S., & Grimell, J. (2025). ADHD and identity formation: Adolescents' experiences from the healthcare system and peer relationships. *Journal of Attention Disorders*, 29(7), 541–553. https://doi.org/10.1177/10870547251318484.

22. Corrigan, P. W., Larson, J. E., & Rüsch, N. (2009). Self-stigma and the "why try" effect: Impact on life goals and evidence-based practices. *World Psychiatry*, 8(2), 75–81. https://doi.org/10.1002/j.2051-5545.2009.tb00218.x.

23. Busby Grant, J., Bruce, C. P., & Batterham, P. J. (2016). Predictors of personal, perceived and self-stigma towards anxiety and depression. *Epidemiology and Psychiatric Sciences*, 25(3), 247–254. https://doi.org/10.1017/s2045796015000220.

24. Darlow, B., Fullen, B. M., Dean, S., Hurley, D. A., Baxter, G. D., & Dowell, A. (2013), The association between health care professional attitudes and beliefs and the attitudes and beliefs, clinical management, and outcomes of patients with low back pain: A systematic review, *European Journal of Pain*, 16(1), 3–17, https://doi.org/10.1016/j.ejpain.2011.06.006; Bunzli, S., Smith, A., Schütze, R., & O'Sullivan, P. (2015), Beliefs underlying pain-related fear and how they evolve: A qualitative investigation in people with chronic back pain and high pain-related fear, *BMJ Open*, 5(10), e008847, https://doi.org/10.1136/bmjopen-2015-008847.

25. Naslund, J. A., Aschbrenner, K. A., Marsch, L. A., & Bartels, S. J. (2016), The future of mental health care: Peer-to-peer support and social media, *Epidemiology and Psychiatric Sciences*, 25(2), 113–122, https://doi.org/10.1017/s2045796015001067; Dunn, S., & Andrews, E. E. (2015), Person-first and identity-first language: Developing psychologists' cultural competence using disability language, *American Psychologist*, 70(3), 255–264, https://doi.org/10.1037/a0038636.

26. Davidson, L., Bellamy, C., Guy, K., & Miller, R. (2012), Peer support among persons with severe mental illnesses: A review of evidence and experience, *World Psychiatry*, 11(2), 123–128, https://doi.org/10.1016/j.wpsyc.2012.05.009; Mead, S., Hilton, D., & Curtis, L. (2001), Peer support: A theoretical perspective, *Psychiatric Rehabilitation Journal*, 25, 134–141, https://doi.org/10.1037/h0095032.

27. Haslam, N. (2016). Concept creep: Psychology's expanding concepts of harm and pathology. *Psychological Inquiry*, 27(1), 1–17. https://doi.org/10.1080/1047840X.2016.1082418.

28. Urwin, R. (May 4, 2025). Majority in UK now 'self-identify' as neurodivergent. *The Sunday Times*. https://www.thetimes.co.uk/uk/science/article/self-diagnose-neurodivergent-99l9kl8v5.

29. Aftab, A. (May 23, 2019). Conversations in critical psychiatry: Allen Frances, MD. *Psychiatric Times*, 36(10). https://www.psychiatrictimes.com/view/conversations-critical-psychiatry-allen-frances-md.

30. Bellet, B. W., Jones, P. J., & McNally, R. J. (2018). Trigger warning: Empirical evidence ahead. *Journal of Behavior Therapy and Experimental Psychiatry*, 61, 134-141. https://doi.org/10.1016/j.jbtep.2018.07.002.

31. Bernard, J. D., Whittles, R. L., Kertz, S. J., & Burke, P. A. (2015). Trauma and event centrality: Valence and incorporation into identity influence well-being more than exposure. *Psychological Trauma: Theory, Research, Practice, and Policy*, 7(1), 11–17. https://psycnet.apa.org/doi/10.1037/a0037331.

32. Stevens, S. K., Timmer-Murillo, S. C., Tomas, C. W., Boals, A., Larson, C. L., deRoon-Cassini, T., et al. (2022). Event centrality and posttraumatic stress symptoms after traumatic injury. *Journal of Traumatic Stress*, 35(6), 1734–1743. https://doi.org/10.1002/jts.22877.

33. Chris (October 2024). Personal communication.

34. Loftus, E. F., & Pickrell, J. E. (1995). The formation of false memories. *Psychiatric Annals*, 25(12), 720–725. https://psycnet.apa.org/doi/10.3928/0048-5713-19951201-07.

35. Wade, K. A., Garry, M., Read, J. D., & Lindsay, D. S. (2002). A picture is worth a thousand lies: Using false photographs to create false childhood memories. *Psychonomic Bulletin & Review*, 9(3), 597–603. https://doi.org/10.3758/bf03196318.

36. Jaroff, L. (November 29, 1993). Repressed-memory therapy: Lies of the mind. *Time*. https://time.com/archive/6724316/repressed-memory-therapy-lies-of-the-mind.

37. Otgaar, H., Howe, M. L., Patihis, L., Merckelbach, H., Lynn, S. J., Lilienfeld, S. O., et al. (2019). The return of the repressed: The persistent and troubling presence of repressed memory in psychology and public discourse. *Perspectives on Psychological Science*, 14(6), 1072–1095. https://doi.org/10.1177/1745691619862306.

38. Marino, G. (February 16, 2025). Professor's little helper. *Psyche*. https://psyche.co/stories-of-change/i-made-professor-before-ritalin-now-i-cant-work-without-it.

39. Covey, S. R. (1989). *The 7 Habits of Highly Effective People*. Free Press.

40. DeRubeis, R. J., Hollon, S. D., Amsterdam, J. D., Shelton, R. C., Young, P. R., Salomon, R. M., et al. (2005). Cognitive therapy vs. medications in the treatment of moderate to severe depression. *Archives of General Psychiatry*, 62(4), 409–416. https://doi.org/10.1001/archpsyc.62.4.409.

41. Otto, M. W., Smits, J. A. J., & Reese, H. E. (2010), Combined psychotherapy and pharmacotherapy for mood and anxiety disorders in adults: Review and analysis, *Focus*, 4(2), 204–214, https://doi.org/10.1176/foc.4.2.204; Swanson, J. M., Arnold, L. E., Molina, B. S. G., Sibley, M. H., Hechtman, L. T., Hinshaw, S. P., et al. (2017), Young adult outcomes in the follow-up of the multimodal treatment study of attention-deficit/hyperactivity disorder: Symptom persistence, source discrepancy, and height suppression, *Journal of Child Psychology and Psychiatry*, 58(6), 663–678, https://doi.org/10.1111/jcpp.12684; Pelham, W. E., Jr., Fabiano, G. A., Waxmonsky, J. G., Greiner, A. R., Gnagy, E. M., Pelham, W. E., III, et al. (2016), Treatment sequencing for childhood ADHD: A multiple-randomization study of adaptive medication and behavioral interventions, *Journal of Clinical Child & Adolescent Psychology*, 45(4), 396–415, https://doi.org/10.1080/15374416.2015.1105138; Daley, D., van der Oord, S., Ferrin, M., Danckaerts, M., Doepfner, M., Cortese, S., et al. (2014), Behavioral interventions in attention-deficit/hyperactivity disorder: A meta-analysis of randomized controlled trials across multiple outcome domains, *Journal of the American Academy of Child & Adolescent Psychiatry*, 53(8), 835–847, https://doi.org/10.1016/j.jaac.2014.05.013.

42. Haig, M. (@MattZHaig) (September 24, 2024). "on an individual level, it can be dangerous to set ourselves in stone." Instagram, reply to Matt Haig. https://www.instagram.com/p/DATyUtnsQXz/f.

Chapter 11. Good Beliefs, Bad Beliefs

1. Bowler, K. (May 11, 2020). Hope wears sneakers. *Everything Happens with Kate Bowler* [podcast]. https://katebowler.com/podcasts/david-fajgenbaum-hope-wears-sneakers.

2. Dispenza, J. (2017). *Becoming Supernatural: How Common People Are Doing the Uncommon*. Hay House.

3. Horowitz, M. (2009). *Occult America: The Secret History of How Mysticism Shaped Our Nation*. Bantam.

4. Peale, N. V. (1952). *The Power of Positive Thinking*. Prentice-Hall.

5. Byrne, R. (2006). *The Secret*. Atria Books.

6. Lyubomirsky, S., Sheldon, K. M., & Schkade, D. (2005), Pursuing happiness: The architecture of sustainable change, *Review of General Psychology*, 9(2), 111–131, https://doi.org/10.1037/1089-2680.9.2.111; Wood, A. M., Perunovic, W. Q. E., & Lee, J. W. (2009), Positive self-statements: Power for some, peril for others, *Psychological Science*, 20(7), 860–866; McNulty, J. K., & Fincham, F. D. (2012), Beyond positive psychology? Toward a contextual view of psychological processes and well-being, *American Psychologist*, 67(2), 101–110, https://doi.org/10.1037/a0024572.

7. Ehrenreich, B. (2009), *Bright-Sided: How the Relentless Promotion of Positive Thinking Has Undermined America*, Metropolitan Books; Sweeney, K., & Shepperd, J. A. (2010), The costs of optimism and the benefits of pessimism, *Emotion*, 10(5), 750–753, https://doi.org/10.1037/a0019016.

8. Oettingen, G. (2014). *Rethinking Positive Thinking: Inside the New Science of Motivation*. Current.

9. Oettingen, G., & Mayer, D. (2002). The motivating function of thinking about the future: Expectations versus fantasies. *Journal of Personality and Social Psychology*, 83(5), 1198–1212.

10. Sidney, A. (1698). *Discourses Concerning Government*. Thomas Bassett.

11. Fajgenbaum, D. (2021). *Chasing My Cure: A Doctor's Race to Turn Hope into Action*. Ballantine Books.

12. Oettingen, G. (2001). Self-regulation of goal-setting: Turning free fantasies about the future into binding goals. *Journal of Personality and Social Psychology*, 80(5), 736–753. http://dx.doi.org/10.1037//0022-3514.80.5.736.

13. Weiner, S. (September 24, 2024). This doctor saved his own life. Now he's on a mission to save thousands more. *AAMCNews*. https://www.aamc.org/news/doctor-saved-his-own-life-now-he-s-mission-save-thousands-more.